Successful Teaching Placements in Secondary Schools

Successful Teaching Placements in Secondary Schools

Editors: Kate Shilvock and Melanie Pope

LearningMatters

First published in 2008 by Learning Matters Ltd.

British Library Cataloguing in Publication Data
A CIP record for this book is available from the British Library.

ISBN 978 1 84445 183 8

Cover design by Code 5 Design Associates Ltd
Project management by Deer Park Productions, Tavistock, Devon
Typeset by PDQ Typesetting Ltd
Printed and bound in Great Britain by Bell& Bain Ltd, Glasgow

Learning Matters Ltd
33 Southernhay East
Exeter EX1 1NX
Tel: 01392 215560
info@learningmatters.co.uk
www.learningmatters.co.uk

Contents

The editors and contributors

Kate Shilvock is an Associate Professor at the Institute of Education, University of Warwick. Kate has led the secondary PGCE core professional studies course and currently leads the secondary PGCE English with drama course. She also has involvement with Graduate Teacher Programme trainees. A former head of English, she has extensive experience of teaching. She has acted as both subject and professional mentor to ITE students on school placement. Kate has interests in literacy and gender issues. She is co-author of a teacher resource *Cross Curricular Literacy 11–14*, Letts (2003) and a contributor to a text for trainee teachers, *Preparing to Teach in Secondary Schools*, Brooks, Abbott and Bills (eds), Open University Press (2004).

Melanie Pope is an Assistant Professor at the Institute of Education, University of Warwick, where she teaches on the secondary PGCE course. She has experience teaching in schools, colleges and universities, and has been a literacy co-ordinator and leading teacher. Melanie's research interests include children's and teachers' metalinguistic awareness and the emotional implications of learning.

Ann Barnes leads the secondary PGCE programme at the University of Warwick and co-ordinates the Modern Foreign Languages (MFL) strand. Her research interests focus on the development of student teachers, particularly in modern languages, assessment in MFL and primary languages. She has published numerous articles, chapters and books in these areas. Ann taught in 11–18 and post-16 institutions before moving into teacher education and supervises a number of research students.

David Curtis taught English in secondary schools in Exeter, Swindon and Blandford Forum before becoming Head of English at Kennett School, Thatcham. He was inspector for English and curriculum for Solihull LEA for 20 years. David has published two books: *Taking Initiatives*, a teachers' book, for Nelson, and *Teaching Secondary English* for Open University Press. David currently works with the secondary PGCE CPS and English with Drama courses at the University of Warwick.

Rachel Dickinson leads the secondary PGCE Drama with English course at the University of Warwick. She also works as a freelance artist educator. Her special interests are in exploring the role of drama in school improvement and devising theatre with and for young people. She is the co-author of a text for drama teachers working in the primary sector.

Marilyn Hunt is Associate Professor in Modern Foreign Languages (Teacher Education) at the University of Warwick. She was head of languages faculty in a comprehensive school where she taught French and Spanish. Her research interests include primary MFL teaching and assessment.

Brian Sanderson is a teaching fellow at the University of Warwick where he leads the secondary PGCE economics and business studies course. An advanced skills teacher, he has considerable experience of teaching in secondary schools.

Susan Shaw co-ordinates training and assessment within the University of Warwick's Graduate Teacher Programme for school-based trainees. She was deputy headteacher within secondary comprehensive schools in Staffordshire, and in Leicestershire. Her responsibilities in school centred around professional development for teaching staff and ITT trainees, development planning and the management of the tutorial system.

Jude Slama leads the secondary PGCE ICT course at the University of Warwick and teaches ICT at an inner-city comprehensive specialist arts school in Birmingham. She has extensive experience of developing teachers' professional competences and led a successful ICT department in a suburban comprehensive school before moving to her current post. Her previous work includes collaborative work on books which focus on practical teaching of ICT.

Introduction

This book is intended for those who want to teach in the secondary phase: Key Stages 3, 4 and post-16 (ages 11–18).

To become a qualified teacher in England and Wales you have to obtain Qualified Teacher Status (QTS) by meeting the relevant professional standards. This is the aim of your initial teacher training (ITT). Following ITT, QTS is confirmed when you successfully complete an induction year in school. An important part of your training will be the time you spend in school on professional placement. This book aims to support you during this so that the experience is successful.

Routes to QTS and professional placement in school

There is a variety of routes you could take to gain QTS. All involve an Initial Teacher Training Provider (ITTP) which arranges and oversees the training programme and assessment of meeting the standards for QTS. The ITTP designs the training plan to be followed. In many cases the ITTP will be a university or Higher Education Institute (HEI) working in a partnership with a group of schools, but in some cases the training provider will only involve a school or schools. No matter what route you are following, you will need to meet the same standards to achieve QTS. This book supports your training and will be useful to you on all of the following routes to QTS.

Post Graduate Certificate in Education/Professional Graduate Certificate in Education (PGCE)

This is the route followed by the largest number of secondary teacher trainees. Most secondary PGCE courses have a university or HEI as the ITTP. These courses are normally of one year duration. The postgraduate route is a Masters level course and will confer Masters level credits which can be 'banked' towards a full Masters degree qualification completed at a later date. A large proportion of the PGCE (roughly two-thirds) is spent on placement.

Employment-based initial teacher training (EBITT)

There are a number of routes which allow the trainee teacher to spend all of the time they are training in school.

1. School-Centred Initial Teacher Training (SCITT). Training, leading to the award of QTS, is based in a school or group of schools and is delivered by practising teachers. These courses are often tailored towards local needs. You will spend most of your time in one school but may have placements in other schools in the consortia. Courses are usually of one year duration.

2. Graduate Teacher Programme (GTP) is 'on the job' training, where trainees qualify whilst working in a school. It is a route often taken by mature trainees who want to change career and continue earning whilst training. You will spend most of your time in one school with short placements in other schools, and will build up your subject knowledge and teaching skills whilst working. Training is usually up to one year duration.

3. Registered Teacher Programme (RTP) is similar to GTP but is aimed at those who have not completed a degree but have some experience of higher education. If you take this route, usually of two years' duration, you will combine school-based training with academic study and complete your degree whilst gaining QTS.

4. Overseas Trained Teacher Programme (OTTP) is for those who have qualified to teach outside the European Economic Area. Overseas-trained teachers have four years in which to gain QTS. Training is completed whilst working in a school.

5. Teach First is for 'top' graduates and is designed to combine training to teach with gaining leadership training and work experience with leading employers. If you follow this route, you will receive a short, intensive training period (a few weeks) and will then spend two years teaching in a challenging secondary school in London, Manchester or the West Midlands.

6. Some universities offer undergraduates the opportunity to take part in the Student Associates Scheme (SAS). Whilst studying for an undergraduate degree, students are able to gain some training in teaching skills and undertake a short placement in school. You do not have to commit to entering teacher training at the end of your degree course, but many who have undertaken SAS do so and can gain some credit for their prior experience.

Undergraduate degree with QTS

If you have not yet gained a degree you may follow an undergraduate degree course of three or four years' duration that includes QTS. You will be awarded a BA, BSc or BEd degree. Your academic study in the university will be interspersed with a number of school placements over the duration of the course.

The standards for the award of QTS and professional placements

The standards for the award of QTS were revised in 2007 and form part of a continuum of professional standards detailing the career stages a teacher might follow. Each set of standards builds on those of an earlier career stage. The Q Standards for the award of QTS are the first of these stages. Having met the Q Standards and successfully completed the induction year, you will progress to the C (Core) Standards for main-scale teachers.

The standards, for all stages, are divided into three, interrelated, sections:

- professional attributes;
- professional knowledge and understanding;
- professional skills.

These are the standards you need to meet in order to gain QTS. Most of them can be demonstrated during your placements. You, and your mentors and tutors, will be using these to set targets and monitor your progress. Your course will be designed to enable you to demonstrate that you have met the QTS Standards but it is your responsibility to gather the evidence. So, you will need to become very familiar with the standards.

Each course is different and your course documentation will suggest how you should keep this evidence and what is appropriate. However, you will find some useful advice and examples given by the Teacher Development Agency (TDA) on their website, listed at the end of this introduction.

Additional placement experiences

There may be other short placements that you undertake to give you experiences that may not be possible in your placement schools. Many training routes require you to undertake an observation placement at the beginning of the course. You may visit a primary school to see Key Stage 2 work in action, to understand the methods, standard of work and transition issues. You may visit a school which demonstrates good practice in teaching children with special educational needs (SEN) or English as an additional language (EAL), or which allows you to observe provision at post-16, if your placement(s) do not offer this. You will not be expected to teach during these placements, but to observe carefully to gain insights which will impact upon your own teaching in your placement school(s).

Beyond QTS

Remember that while gaining QTS is your focus for the duration of your training, it is just the beginning of your development as a teacher. It is important that you recognise that you will have a lot to learn once you take up your first post, and part of your professional responsibilities is to be responsible for your own continuing professional development (CPD), both through your induction year (a period of one year full-time of school-based training when you are an NQT), and beyond into your career.

How to use this book

This book is designed to support you during your professional placements. It is intended to complement your training, and to provide a practical resource that you can turn to in order to develop your skills, or when you are having difficulties, or when you are not sure how to act when you are working in your professional placements. You should continue to read widely around your subject pedagogy and other critical readings during each placement to ensure that the development of your basic classroom skills is supported by increased understanding of pedagogy and subject knowledge.

Depending on your ITT programme, you will undertake one or more professional placements during your training period – this varies according to the route you are taking. For simplicity, throughout the book we refer to time in school as 'placement'. The chapters are designed to be revisited by you at various stages in your training, and indicate tasks and sections that are relevant to later stages of training and development as 'moving on', to enable you to focus on your progress towards QTS. There is no set point at which you should move on to these areas; it will depend on your individual progress and development through your training.

PRACTICAL TASK PRACTICAL TASK PRACTICAL TASK PRACTICAL TASK PRACTICAL TASK

Before you go any further in this book, and at the very start of each placement or stage in your training, you should review a number of important documents.

- Your training handbook from your ITT provider. Make sure you know what is happening at each stage of your training, and what is expected of you during each placement.

- Your ITT plan (this may be called your training record, professional development portfolio, monitoring file, etc.). This will contain personal information about you and your training, including reports and targets. Consider what strengths you will be taking into the beginning of your training.

- The standards for the award of QTS (Q Standards only, see Useful websites below). You will get to know them very well during your training, but at this point you will need to familiarise yourself with them so that you have an idea of what you have to do to gain QTS.

A SUMMARY OF **KEY POINTS**

> Placements will vary according to the training route you have chosen. Make sure you understand what is required of you, and the pattern of your school placement(s).

> Make sure you become familiar with your training plan and the professional standards for the award of QTS.

> Placement will enable you to demonstrate your achievement of the standards for the award of QTS.

> Refer to your course documentation for information on how to demonstrate achievement of the standards for the award of QTS.

Useful websites

TDA Professional Standards

www.tda.gov.uk/teachers/professionalstandards.aspx

Make sure you look at the standards marked 'Q' for people qualifying to teach. The other standards relate to qualified teachers in post.

TDA QTS Standards guidance

www.tda.gov.uk/partners/ittstandards/guidance_08/qts.aspx?keywords=standards+guidance This document helps you to understand how you demonstrate evidence of having met the standards.

Coverage of QTS Standards in this book

This grid indicates which Q Standards are covered in which chapters, for ease of reference at different stages in your training.

Q Standard	Chapters											
	1	**2**	**3**	**4**	**5**	**6**	**7**	**8**	**9**	**10**	**11**	**12**
1		✓			✓		✓	✓				
2		✓					✓	✓				
3	✓		✓					✓	✓	✓		
4	✓	✓	✓		✓		✓	✓				
5		✓					✓	✓				
6	✓	✓								✓		
7		✓		✓	✓				✓		✓	✓
8					✓					✓	✓	
9		✓			✓						✓	
10				✓	✓		✓					
11						✓						
12						✓						
13			✓			✓						
14					✓							
15									✓	✓		
16	Skills tests											
17										✓		
18									✓	✓		
19				✓						✓		
20	✓											
21							✓	✓				
22					✓							
23					✓							
24					✓	✓						
25					✓							
26						✓						
27						✓						
28						✓						
29				✓	✓						✓	
30			✓				✓					
31							✓					
32	✓	✓	✓	✓						✓	✓	
33											✓	

1
Orientation: preparing for placement

By the end of this chapter you should:

- understand how your teaching placements are organised;
- know what you need to do in order to prepare effectively for your placements;
- be able to organise yourself and your resources in readiness for the placements;
- understand what is to be gained by focused observation of others' teaching.

This chapter addresses the following Professional Standards for QTS:

Q3(a,b), Q4, Q6, Q20, Q32

Introduction

The purpose of this chapter is to help you be as prepared as possible prior to starting your professional teaching placements. Once a placement is under way, it is very challenging to make up for lost time if you were unprepared at the beginning – thoughtful and thorough preparation in advance will help you in your development as a teacher and will contribute to a more successful placement, both for you and your pupils as well as the other staff involved in your development. This is the case whether it is the first time you have started a placement in school or whether you have already completed one. As you are aware, each school is different.

How your placements are organised

When you receive notification of your placement, you may initially wonder why you have been allocated a particular school. There are many factors which have to be taken into account when placing you on a professional placement, some of the most important being:

- your particular training needs (e.g. age range of pupils, specific subject, contrast to a previous placement, etc.);
- where you live and whether you have transport or transport is available;
- the provision at the school (e.g. trained mentors, etc.).

Even if you know of a nearer school, this does not mean it would be a suitable placement for you and your needs. Usually, the school will need to be in partnership with your ITTP and will have trained the teachers to act as mentors for you in your development as a teacher.

Understanding the school context

When you know the name and location of your school, it is professional to find out as much relevant information as you can before you start your placement. The sources of this information can (and should) be both official and less formal. Try not to base your opinion on preconceived ideas about a school's perceived reputation, whether positive or negative, or the area in which it is located.

You should consult the following sources.

- Official sources of information such as Office for Standards in Education (Ofsted) reports and Department for Children, Schools and Families (DCSF) data. However, such information needs to be treated with caution, as, for example, an Ofsted report could be perhaps two years old and a great deal could have changed since then.
- The school's website and publicity/information brochures.
- Your tutors and colleagues.
- Other internet sites that provide information about a school's performance, e.g. the comparative data at the BBC Education website on GCSE/A level results as well as CVA (contextual value-added). Once again, however, be careful how you approach this type of data: it is usually 'whole school' and may not reflect the department you will be working in.

If possible, go to see the school so you can really get a feel for it – the size, type of buildings, amenities, access, etc. It would also be a good idea to drive (or preferably walk) around the catchment area and find out where your pupils are coming from, what facilities are available, etc. If you are going to do a trial journey to find out how long it will take, be aware that traffic is much heavier on a school day and parking will probably be very difficult. You need to arrive punctually.

The type of school where you are placed may vary considerably when you compare your school with those of peers. There are many different types of school, and you need to be clear on what to expect from your placement. Is it:

- state-maintained or independent?
- mixed or single sex?
- selective or comprehensive?
- 11–16, 11–18, 14–19?
- faith school or secular?
- a school with a specialist status? If so, what?
- a trust or academy school?
- does the school have any particular features, e.g. vertical tutoring, adopting a 'house' system (see Chapter 8), etc?
- how are classes organised – mixed ability, banding, streaming, setting (see Chapter 10)?

Whatever information you collate should enable you to ask effective questions when you arrive, as well as ensuring that you appear (and indeed are) professionally informed.

What to expect

There is a variety of models in existence for professional teaching placements, depending on the training route you are following, and whether you are training full- or part-time – and of course if you are training via an employment-based route, your job will be your 'placement', although you may have opportunities to undertake short placements in different schools . So, some placements are relatively short and take place earlier or later in the training year; others are longer and occur mainly in the main part of the school year, or are the full length of the school year. It is crucial that you are aware of exactly what expectations are demanded of you during your placements. For example, check the following.

- How much of a teaching timetable are you expected to teach and when are you expected to start with this?
- Are you expected to teach across the full age range of the school?
- Will you be introduced to teaching gradually (e.g. through observation, to small-group work, to planning and teaching certain 'slots', to teaching full lessons alone)?
- Will you be 'paired' with another trainee (i.e. will you share some classes, plan together, etc.)?
- Are you expected to carry out various professional/academic tasks whilst on placement (e.g. collecting information about the assessment procedures, conducting a small-scale research project, finding out about, e.g. special educational needs procedures, etc.)?
- Find out which members of staff will have responsibility for your training, and their roles.
- How often will you be expected to meet with them?
- What evidence should you keep to demonstrate achievement of the Q Standards?
- Are there specific forms/portfolios/tasks you need to complete during your placement? If so, when and how regularly? Are these to be assessed, and if so, when and how? Can you plan ahead?
- Will you be attached to a form, i.e. will you have a pastoral role?
- ICT access? Will you be provided with a laptop or given access to the school computer network?

The roles of people involved in your placement

The titles for the various people will differ depending upon your particular ITTP training route (see Introduction for alternative titles), but you should be aware of the usual roles and responsibilities of the following people. It is usually the case that all of the following will observe your teaching (including the whole range of your professional activities, including e.g. meetings, reporting, etc.) during your placements and will try to provide constructive feedback. Regular observation and monitoring are aspects you will need to become accustomed to, and an understanding of others' roles and responsibilities should help you.

Your subject mentor

This person is directly in charge of your day-to-day planning, teaching and assessment in your particular subject(s) and for your subject knowledge development. They will usually plan your timetable, liaise with other members of the department, meet regularly with you to discuss your progress and ensure you have information such as schemes of work, resources, etc. The subject mentor will play a key role in your development as a teacher. It is crucial you develop a positive working relationship with him or her (see Chapter 2): this person will help set your targets, monitor your progress, etc. Be mindful that they will also have to do the rest of their job.

Your professional/whole-school mentor

This person usually has an overview of all beginning teachers in the school and often co-ordinates a professional programme for trainees. This person also monitors the work of the subject mentors and ensures communications with your ITTP are effective. They are frequently also responsible for arranging your pastoral attachment or programme, e.g. to a form group. Your professional mentor is often a member of the leadership team and may have a very wide range of responsibilities. They should be a useful source of help and support for you, but again, you need to be aware of other demands on their time.

Your (visiting) subject tutor

This person is usually based in an ITTP and works with you and your subject mentor on your development as a teacher. They will visit you during your placement and observe your teaching, often jointly with the subject mentor or class teacher. They will provide constructive feedback on your progress and development, and will help set you targets in consultation with your subject mentor and you. They can often provide a more decontextualised picture than of the particular school issues.

Other visiting tutors

It may also be the case that your ITTP requires that another tutor visits the school during your placement, probably to liaise with your professional mentor, and sometimes to observe you teach, perhaps for moderation purposes. You may also be visited by an external examiner, often from another ITTP. This is usually either as part of a sample for moderation, or because you may be on the pass/fail borderline, and another opinion is required.

All these people are sources of support, advice and help during your placement.

Before you start

It is always advisable as a trainee teacher to join a professional association (union). It is usually the case that you are able to join all the unions at least in your training year for free. Joining these associations will be of help to you if something should go seriously wrong during your placement (it very rarely does), and their websites and materials will help you become familiar with your legal rights and responsibilities as a teacher. Relevant addresses are to be found at the end of this chapter. You can consult the websites for the following task. Your ITTP may incorporate a session at which each association introduces itself; if not, consult the website or, better still, staff in school (there are often union representatives on the staff).

PRACTICAL TASK PRACTICAL TASK PRACTICAL TASK PRACTICAL TASK PRACTICAL TASK

Find out from any sources available to you:

- your legal position if you are left alone with a class;
- what you should do if a pupil confides in you about something potentially serious;
- what you should do if you suspect a pupil is being bullied;
- what your legal rights and responsibilities are regarding the school and national codes for the safety and well-being of pupils in your charge, e.g. management of behaviour.

REFLECTIVE TASK
REFLECTIVE TASK

Consider how prepared you are at this point in your training to deal with any of the above issues. Make a list of questions and training needs to take to your next meeting with your tutor or mentor.

Moving on

Reflect on occasions when you have had to deal with any of the above issues during training. How would you change the way you dealt with it, and why?

Forward planning: paperwork and procedures

As was mentioned above, there are probably a great number and range of forms, tasks, assignments, files and lists to complete during your placement. Whatever you do, make sure you know what is expected from you, and when. You should then do two things.

- List the documents and the dates (perhaps in the form of Table 1.1).
- Work backwards from when the various items need to be completed/handed in/collected and note in your diary when and how you are going to achieve each one.

Table 1.1

Document/task/where is it?	Date required	Who/what can help me/ provide me with information	What I need to do now
Example: tutorial form with subject mentor (in my professional development folder)	By 15 November	Subject mentor	Need to arrange convenient time to meet
Example: subject assignment on assessment (details in my subject handbook)	By 6 January	Subject mentor and subject tutor	Need to identify a class homework task to analyse and write up
Example: professional task on reporting to parents (details in my professional studies handbook)	By 8 February	Professional mentor/school documentation	Need to find out how the school system is set up

You will save yourself time and stress by ensuring as much as possible is in place before you begin your full teaching timetable. This will include, for example, setting up a file for each class you will teach, including class list, previous assessment details, relevant scheme of work, resources, etc. It will also help if you have (electronically and in hard copy as appropriate) a sufficient supply of lesson plan pro formas, observation schedules, etc.

Gathering information

In some cases, you will have a chance to meet your mentor before you start your placement, in which case it is very helpful to collate as much information about the department and the school as you can. The following sections provide some ideas for what you might find useful.

Information on your pupils

Your classes will have already been 'assessed' by their teacher (both formatively and summatively). Any data that is already available will help you in terms of planning your lessons. It is important you have access to all information that is available to the class teacher for all the classes you are going to be planning for, teaching and assessing. Find out what baseline data is used by the school and what target-setting process is being used (see Chapter 3).

Information on schemes of work, exam specifications, etc.

Departments normally have schemes of work (SoW) in place. However, you may be asked to prepare your own, but you should be given some guidance for this. It is reasonable to use the department's SoW as a basis for your own work. See Chapter 4 for further information on planning.

It is also important to find out what the future examination/assessment programme is for your classes. If they have internal or external tests coming up this needs to be reflected in your lesson planning. If the groups are in KS4 or KS5, find out which examining group is being used if you can, and then access the appropriate website for past papers, mark schemes, etc. Check to see which resources the department has, and which sections you need copies of.

Information on whole-school policies

To ensure you are as prepared as possible, and that you are able to act in a professional, assured manner when in school, being familiar with policies on such matters as assessment, code of behaviour, reward and sanction systems and homework expectations will stand you in good stead. Handing out detentions when pupils know it is not deserved or does not follow the school's policy concerning warnings is not the best recipe for motivated classes who are keen to learn. Doing your own 'homework' in advance of the placement can make this less likely.

Preparing specific subject knowledge requirements

If at all possible, ascertaining what the subject knowledge requirements are for the classes you are going to teach on your placement will make your preparation much clearer. You will need to identify which areas you feel confident in, and which you are less sure of. Make the most of contacts before your placement to try to fill any gaps in your own subject knowledge, as well as ideas on how to teach certain topics. Some suggestions are below.

- Access the key textbooks in the areas you need to be familiar with (many of these are endorsed by examining groups or written by chief examiners – this at least gives you a feeling of security about the subjects covered).
- Websites are another invaluable source of support materials and guidance, but you should be careful and be selective. You will usually be aware of your professional subject association, which will have up to date resources and ideas for teaching and learning. 'Commercial' websites are often 'resource rich' and can in theory save a great deal of time, but beware: you will need to adapt to your own needs and those of your learners. Another popular website is the BBC which supports most subject areas, with sections like Bitesize being very popular.
- It is of great benefit when a group of student teachers pools resources prior to and during placements. This can be an excellent source of support and inspiration for you: 'using' someone else's resource or idea is not always at all straightforward (you will adapt it to your own style, the context and needs of your learners, etc.) but it can start you off thinking how to approach a topic or a problem and can therefore be a real help when you are tired, exhausted or stuck for ideas.

Making the most of initial observations of teaching

When you first begin a placement, you will usually be offered the opportunity to observe other teachers' lessons. Make the most of these. (NB: when you are teaching your own timetable, it is also very helpful to carry on observing, since you continue to learn a lot about your own practice.) The following are quotations from trainee teachers. How do you react personally to each one?

> *It is good to see the style of teaching, i.e. what you have to follow. It makes you prepared for any comments pupils make on your style/approach. It gives an idea of the amount of material actually covered!*

> *I find observing lessons extremely useful as it gives the opportunity to observe various teaching styles and to get plenty of ideas on 'games' and classroom management techniques.*

> *I find that observation or being 'told' about things is useful but a bit 'on the outside looking in'.*

> *The lessons I observed at the school enabled me to get a good feel of the departmental policy in matters such as discipline strategies, approaches with reluctant learners, disruptive pupils, good pupils. It allowed me to get a feel for the strategies I may have needed throughout my placement.*

If you make good use of observation, you should feel the benefits (rather than the restrictions felt by one of the trainees cited above), where you learn from what you observe, reflect on it and decide how your observations influence your development. Observation should never be boring: you should learn something from every observation (like the other quotations), and that can be helped by having a clear focus. It should also not be the case that you restrict your observations to your own subject area: try to arrange observations in a variety of subjects with a variety of teaching styles. It is worth asking the following questions.

- What has been put in place beforehand (equipment, resources etc.)?
- How does the teacher get the attention of the class initially?
- How does the teacher express high expectations of the class?
- How does the teacher get the class to change direction/to move from one activity to another?
- How does the teacher stop the activities?
- What exactly is on pupils' desks at various points in the lesson? What opportunities do pupils have to 'fiddle', etc.?
- When pupils have finished, do they have something to do? Do they have any routine, e.g. learning, practising, etc.?
- How does the teacher check all pupils have understood?
- If ICT is used, how does this enhance the learning?
- How is praise used? Publicly? Privately?
- How was the pace and variety achieved?
- Did the teacher have access to any support from other adults? How was this used?
- Was questioning used effectively?
- How was differentiation incorporated/were the needs of all pupils catered for?
- How did the teacher show awareness/peripheral vision? (i.e. could you see how this led to preventative classroom management).

It is, of course, not the case that you will see all the above exemplified in every lesson you observe. In some cases, you will be able to reflect on one area more than another; in some cases, it could be that the lack of one area of focus may lead you to reflect on the reasons for it, or its impact.

At the end of each lesson you observe, you might ask yourself the following questions:

- What were the short-term objectives? What were the overall aims?
- How were the differing needs of pupils met?
- What was most successful and why?
- How did the teacher deal with any problems that arose (behaviour, misunderstandings, etc.)?
- Did learning take place? (After all, this is clearly the crucial factor.)
- What have you learnt? (ideas, activities, strategies – both positive and negative; changes to how you think you might plan your lessons).

Observation 'etiquette'

It is a privilege to be able to observe others in order to work towards your own professional development. It is vital that you make sure these relationships with colleagues remain as positive as possible. For this reason, it is advisable to make sure you do the following.

- Ensure the person you're observing knows who you are and why you're there.
- Get involved in the lesson only if the teacher says that's OK.
- Make sure you thank them for the chance to observe the lesson.
- Be sensitive to the pressures staff face – they cannot always afford to spend lots of time with you. Remember not to be overcritical of staff, methods, procedures, etc.
- Few lessons are ever perfect. Please bear this in mind when observing teachers and commenting to them afterwards.
- If you make critical comments on your observation pro forma, make sure these remain confidential and constructive.
- Take opportunities where appropriate to become involved (e.g. when pupils are working in pairs or groups). Don't feel that all observation must be done at the back as if you were invisible.
- A smile helps a lot too!

A SUMMARY OF **KEY POINTS**

> **Make sure you understand how your teaching placements are organised and find out as much as you can in advance of what is expected of you.**

> **Find out what you can about your placement school: its context, its expectations, its ethos, etc.**

> **Be as prepared as possible before the placement begins: to have some tasks already done will make your start to the placement so much smoother.**

> **Focus clearly on how you can learn through observations of others' teaching.**

REFERENCES REFERENCES **REFERENCES** REFERENCES **REFERENCES** REFERENCES
BBC Bitesize website www.bbc.co.uk/schools/revision/
Department for Children, Schools and Families (DCSF) www.dfes.gov.uk/
Office for Standards in Education (Ofsted) www.ofsted.gov.uk/

FURTHER READING FURTHER READING **FURTHER READING** FURTHER READING

Brooks, V., Abbott, I. and Bills, L. (eds.) (2007) *Preparing to teach in secondary schools: A student teacher's guide to professional issues in secondary education* (2nd edition). Maidenhead: OUP.

Useful websites

Training and Development Agency for Schools (TDA) www.tda.gov.uk/

Teachernet www.teachernet.gov.uk/

Information on identifying and joining subject associations for teachers
www.subjectassociations.org.uk

2
The challenges of placement

By the end of this chapter you should:

- know what it means to conduct yourself in a professional manner when in school;
- have an understanding of the relationships you will form with your mentor and class teachers when you start placement;
- have considered the pressures of time management and personal organisation.

This chapter addresses the following Professional Standards for QTS:

Q1, Q2, Q4, Q5, Q6, Q7, Q9, Q32

Introduction

The purpose of this chapter is for you to develop an understanding of the relationships you will build with staff and students during your placements. It will also consider some of the key challenges you will face on placement from a very practical viewpoint. This chapter looks specifically at how you can ensure you are prepared to conduct yourself in a professional way prior to starting placement by ensuring you are thoroughly briefed on what is expected of you. In this chapter, you will develop your professional attributes which will help you to prepare for the challenges of becoming a successful teacher.

Professional conduct

In teaching, professionalism is of the utmost importance as it will underpin your reputation with colleagues and students. Professionalism is the manner in which you address others, the manner in which you dress and conduct yourself whilst on school premises as well as the ways in which you express yourself with students, staff and parents. Remaining professional at all times can be difficult, as sometimes you may become frustrated by situations involving students or staff. It is important to make sure that your tone of voice, facial expressions and the words you use are in keeping with what is expected of you as a professional.

How to be professional in dealings with students

In a secondary school, you are judged by students firstly on what they see of you. This is because, until you have established a professional rapport with students, they have very little to go on in terms of knowing that you are a professional. Your first consideration therefore should be how you appear to students. You should consider what to wear and also what not to wear. It is better to appear more formal than too casual as this can be misinterpreted by students as indicative of a less professional approach to your work. You should ensure that your attire is in keeping with that of other staff. For female members of staff, you must ensure that your dress is not too revealing. For male members of staff, most schools expect you to wear a tie and wearing jeans is not generally acceptable. This is more important than you may have considered, as inappropriate attire may result in students' poor concentration and therefore poor learning. It also sends out the wrong message to young people, as you are a role model. In relation to Q2, you are expected to demonstrate the positive values, attitudes and behaviours you expect of students and this starts with your attire and your behaviour when you interact with them.

Another point to consider is how you will address students and how you expect them to address you. It is always best to be respectful of students as they will find it difficult to respect you if they feel you do not respect them. Wherever possible, use students' names when addressing them. Furthermore, you should consider your body language and proximity to students when you interact with them. You should not invade students' personal space as this is very unprofessional. Your body language should be open, friendly and relaxed whilst commanding some measure of authority.

How to be professional in dealings with staff

As it is important to be professional when dealing with students, it is also important for you to be professional when you deal with staff in schools. This extends to all staff, from the receptionist who greets you at the entrance, to the dinner ladies you will meet in the school canteen, and includes all the teachers you will come across in the staffroom and supply staff you will see when regular teachers are away. You should also consider the teaching assistants (TAs) you will work with; you are expected to address them courteously and be professional by informing them of your lesson content and advising them of the role you want them to take on in your lesson.

You should always make sure you extend the same courtesy to any adult in school that you would wish them to extend to you. In fact, it is more important for you to appear polite and professional than it is for them. Remember you are in training whereas they are qualified, experienced and in post. You should make sure that you do not ever comment aloud about any staff member whom you feel has acted inappropriately towards either yourself or a student. The obvious exception here is if you feel there is a child protection issue in which case you have a professional duty to report it through the appropriate channels.

Make an effort to get to know the staff at your placement schools. It is important to show you are keen to fit in.

You should also remember that you may not always see staff at their best, but it is not your place to pass judgement. This extends to comments following a lesson you have observed; discussing with staff how they could improve their delivery is both inappropriate and generally unprofessional. Staff may feel comfortable telling you they know that their lesson was perhaps not a very successful one but they will not expect you to launch into an explanation of how they could have done it better. Remember that they will probably have been teaching for some time and are aware of their strengths and areas for development. Although you are of course expected to integrate into your department and contribute to its development, you are not there to criticise staff lessons or staff interactions with students, and you should take care that you do not make comments that can be inadvertently interpreted as criticisms.

CASE STUDY

Blayne

Blayne was placed in a rural school in which students were particularly difficult as they had little motivation to attend school or succeed educationally. Blayne found that many staff had worked in this school for many years, and that there was a culture of fatalism which meant that staff were not overly concerned by improving standards. Blayne often observed lessons held by a cover teacher who was clearly struggling to find meaningful work for the students to complete. In the staffroom, Blayne remarked innocently to a fellow PGCE trainee that it was a shame the head of department had not provided more work for the cover teacher to set the students as that was clearly a problem during cover lessons. Following this comment, Blayne suddenly found that staff in the department kept their interactions with him to a strict minimum. He was also asked to start working in the staffroom rather than leave his things in the departmental office and was generally made to feel unwelcome around the department. By the time his subject tutor visited the school, Blayne felt very isolated and dejected, having no idea what had taken place. The subject tutor was able to talk to the head of department and find out that Blayne's innocent comments had been repeated with the emphasis put on the fact that there had not been any work provided by the head of department. When Blayne was made aware of this, he was able to apologise and that helped to smooth relations over with his head of department who was also his mentor.

REFLECTIVE TASK

How would it affect you if you lived close to one of your placement schools? How would you act when you met students outside of school contexts? How would you ensure you remained professional in those interactions?

Moving on

What choices will you make about the schools you apply to for your first job? Consider how your experiences of professional conduct will influence this decision.

How to be professional in dealings with parents and carers

First of all, you should be aware that at no point during your placements are you expected to deal with parents or carers without the support of your mentor or a classroom teacher. Indeed, before arranging a meeting with a parent, you should always check with your mentor whether this is appropriate and make sure that your mentor or the class teacher of the student is present at the meeting.

On the phone, it is important to remember that the person on the end of the phone cannot see you and has no idea why you are calling. You should always check with your mentor before you phone a student's parents. If you are going to make a phone call to a parent, make sure you have thought carefully about why you are phoning and what you will say. Make sure you introduce yourself and check that you are speaking to the parent or guardian of the student before you go any further. State clearly both the purpose of your call and what you think the parent can help with.

If you are meeting a parent face to face, it will more than likely be at a parent–teacher consultation evening and you should have the support of a classroom teacher or your mentor to guide you. You should listen to how the teacher interacts with the parent. What do they say? How do they start and end the conversation?

Developing effective working relationships

Relationships with mentors

During your training you will meet a number of different mentors who will have different roles in your training (as outlined in Chapter 1, and see Chapter 3 for your responsibilities to your mentors and others). You will need to establish professional relationships with mentors as quickly as possible. There may also be a training programme of development from a whole-school point of view. The number of meetings you have with mentors will vary from school to school and depend on which phase of your training you are in.

Regardless of how often you see mentors, it is important to understand the relationship you are likely to have with them. One of your mentors may be the head of department or they may be a classroom teacher who has the responsibility for mentoring trainees on placement. In either case, you will need to be aware of what they expect of you.

Mentors will expect you to help them by making the mentoring process as easy as possible for them. They are there to give you guidance and support on how to teach and how to improve your teaching, but they will expect you to be knowledgeable on what paperwork needs completing and who needs to complete it (see Chapter 1). Although you will be very busy on placement, your mentor will be busier and will be preoccupied with many other school issues. It is important to remember that a mentor's time is very limited and they may not always be able to give you the support you would like to receive. In order to make this relationship easier, you should make sure you are proactive in volunteering to help your mentor in whatever ways you can. This includes making sure you take information in the first time you are told something so that the mentor does not need to remind you of things they have already told you.

This is especially important as placement can feel overwhelming at times and you may forget key information which your mentor knows they have communicated to you. Try to keep track of key information by writing it down as you will probably not be able to remember everything you are told. You should keep a notebook to help you record key information. This could be something as small as the date of the next staff training day or the fact that the Year 9 mock SATs are coming up and therefore there will be lots of disruption to Year 9 lessons across the school.

To support the relationship with your mentor, you should make sure you ask the right questions about what lessons you will be teaching and who you will be teaching so that the mentor does not feel they have to constantly give you information. Asking the right questions will show your mentor you are fully aware of what is going on in school and in the department.

You may have a second school mentor who will have more of an overview of your progress and is likely to be a senior teacher within the school structure, such as an assistant head teacher or a deputy head teacher. Remember that to a mentor, supporting you is only one of a number of tasks they need to complete and so they may sometimes not have the time to see you or discuss with you in great depth what you need to do next. This is perfectly normal and you should try wherever possible to accommodate your mentors' busy schedules.

Following on from lesson observations, you should try to ensure that discussion of the good practice which you have noted in terms of learning strategies, and how you can adapt these ideas for your own teaching, becomes a regular feature of developmental meetings with your school mentor. This will help you to develop your practice and to focus discussions with your mentor around key teaching and learning issues.

At first it is almost inevitable that practical management issues will take up much time in these meetings, but if there is a focus on the development of learning from the outset the gains in this respect in terms of positive response from students may well reduce other concerns.

Relationships with class teachers

In most cases, class teachers will be happy to sit down with you and help you plan the series of lessons you are taking on their behalf. The class teacher will offer you valuable feedback at the end of your lessons and they will also give you advice on how to best approach the individual students in their classes.

In order to keep good relations with class teachers you should aim to give them copies of your lesson plans well in advance so that they know what you plan to do with their classes. This will allow class teachers to give you any constructive criticism they think you might need. Also, remember the class teacher knows the students better than you do so they are likely to know what will work best with them.

The class teacher retains responsibility for students' learning, and they may wish to be present until they are aware of how you teach. In some circumstances, a phased introduction to certain groups, until both you and they are sure that learning is going to take place, is appropriate. There are many benefits to phased introduction to groups, including the opportunity to team-teach with more experienced colleagues.

Multiple placements: relationships with other trainees

A model that some ITTPs use, especially during early stages of placement, is that of multiple placements. This is where more than one trainee is placed in the same department and will be allocated shared responsibility for some teaching groups. Some trainees are unhappy about this and perceive it as offering them reduced opportunities for teaching. However, multiple placements are usually very successful in practice, and trainees learn a lot from each other, especially in planning, resourcing, team-teaching and observing or supporting each other.

If you find yourself in a multiple placement, remember that you need to be as professional with the other trainee as you would be with any other member of staff. You must extend the same consideration, organisation, record-keeping and responsibility for delivering what you agree to as you would with any class teacher. Multiple placements tend to go wrong only when one trainee is not delivering their 'share' of the work. Remember that you are still being judged according to your individual ability to meet the standards during a multiple placement, so your performance counts just as much as during a solo placement.

Time management and organisation

One of the greatest challenges of placement is remaining organised and on top of everything. This is particularly difficult if you have external pressures such as part-time employment or family commitments.

Planning lessons can take up an inordinate amount of time. You should be planning at least a few days in advance so that you can show class teachers and mentors your lesson plans before you teach them, so that they have an opportunity to ask you to change the content of the lesson plan if they want to. If you show lesson plans to teachers a few days before lessons, you will find your relationships with those teachers will be improved as they will gain confidence in your abilities to be organised and efficient. They will also have the opportunity to give you feedback and you should still have time to amend your lesson plans as a result of this feedback. This will support your progress.

You should find out as soon as possible what other school pressures you will have. For example, you are expected to mark work whilst on placement and you are expected to attend parents' evenings and write reports.

If you feel it is all getting too much for you, you should speak to your mentor but also contact your ITTP tutor who may be able to help. It is normal to find placement stressful at times. This can be difficult with students, who often know that you are not a permanent member of staff. Make sure you speak to someone if you feel under pressure.

Transition between placements/phases of training

At the start of your training, you may well spend the first few weeks observing lessons in your placement school and very gradually move into teaching lessons with the support of your mentors. As your training progresses, in the later stages, you may find the observation time is reduced and the focus upon arriving at a new placement/taking on new roles or responsibility during placement changes. Make sure you are prepared by finding out as much information as you can about your placement school(s).

You will find during your training that you experience very different situations from one placement to another. You may find the type of school you are placed in is very different, or you may find the staff have a totally different approach from one school to the other. You may find that one of your mentors is very present and wants to spend a lot of time with you going over every detail of your lesson plans, while the next mentor may stand back more and want you to experiment for yourself and allow you to make your own mistakes. You should use the contrast between your school experiences to help you reflect and to enable you to develop and hone your classroom skills.

You should use personal reflection from your placements as a way of considering what you need to do on your next placement to improve your practice. This is especially true in the later stages of your training.

Lesson observations play a key role in facilitating transition between placements. Through focused observation, you will be able to reflect on your own practice and improve considerably. Through your training you should have been introduced to a number of learning strategies – focused peer discussion, scaffolding, moving students through the zone of proximal development (ZPD) by appropriate prompts and questions, the establishment of clear learning objectives and linked investigative tasks, providing for different styles of learning, e.g. visual, auditory and kinaesthetic (VAK), engagement activities which channel ideas and make links in the students' working memories, assessment for learning (AfL), etc. In any given lesson, learning strategies utilised will necessarily be limited, but if you undertake a number of lesson observations each week you should be able to record many good exemplifications.

PRACTICAL TASK PRACTICAL TASK PRACTICAL TASK PRACTICAL TASK PRACTICAL TASK

Use the chart in Table 2.1 to record the good practice noted over the last school week, and continue to highlight well thought out learning strategies as part of your observation records on an ongoing basis.

Table 2.1

Learning strategies	Evidence sought	Details of example observed	Why is it effective?
Focused peer discussion	Structured discussion agenda for pairs, small groups		
Scaffolding	Progressive use of examples Progressive use of learning activities Progressive use of questions		
Zone of Proximal Development (ZPD)	Clear intervention in learning process by peers Clear intervention in learning process by teacher Guided learning for small groups		
Learning objectives and investigative tasks	Clarity in required direction of learning, supported by very well resourced investigative task		
Styles of learning	Finding alternatives from the norm in VAK range Offering alternatives for theoretical, reflective, activist and pragmatic learners Simply offering different approaches to individual or group learning		
Engagement activities	Extending the learning moment by active involvement with factual input		
Using assessment to stimulate learning (AfL)	Involving students in assessment and improvement of learning outcomes on ongoing basis		
Moving on: Other learning strategies . . .			

Whilst you should undertake the majority of your observations within your own department or faculty in order to support your development of specialist pedagogy, it is helpful to seek other foci from time to time – e.g. observations across the curriculum, observations in practical subjects, observations in a particular ability range or key stage – as this will provide you with useful comparisons and new approaches.

Other school experiences

If possible, you should try to take part in the life of the whole school and therefore join in lunchtime or after-school activities when appropriate. Here are some examples of trainees who were able to take part in other activities.

CASE STUDIES
Other school experiences
Case study 1
Carole is a trainee in mathematics. She plays the saxophone and noticed that her placement school has a student jazz band. She asked the music teachers if she could participate in any way and was told she could practise with the jazz band. Through the band, Carole was able to form very productive relationships with some of her difficult Year 11 students who had been misbehaving in her lessons. She found that the students were much more co-operative after she started practising with the jazz band.

Case study 2
Josh is a drama trainee. He overheard a conversation in the staffroom where teachers were discussing the next Duke of Edinburgh trip, saying that they were struggling to find another male member of staff to accompany them on a weekend activity. Josh volunteered himself and went on the trip and had a great time. He decided it was an area to develop when in his first post.

Frequently asked questions

One of the class teachers whose group I teach has told me that I am never to phone the parents of one of my students, but I feel that it is really important that I speak to them as soon as possible. What should I do?

The first thing you must do is respect what the teacher has asked of you. There are sometimes reasons why teachers do not phone the parents of specific students, and it is possible that the class teacher knows the reasons why but has not passed the full information to you. It is imperative that you do not go ahead and call; you should only ever make a phone call once it has been sanctioned by your mentor, so that they can give you appropriate support in doing so. Talk to your mentor about finding alternative ways of dealing with this situation; they will know what strategies have been put in place for this student.

A SUMMARY OF **KEY POINTS**

> **Make sure your conduct and attire are professional, when dealing with both staff and students.**

> **To build effective relationships with mentors and class teachers you need to remember they are very busy and are there to facilitate your placements.**

> Try to be organised in terms of both your training commitments and your lesson planning as this will help you to keep your stress levels to a minimum.

> Get involved in the school's wider activities if you can as this will help you to integrate into the school and will also allow you to interact with students and staff in a different setting.

REFERENCES REFERENCES **REFERENCES** REFERENCES **REFERENCES** REFERENCES

Gardner, H. (1993) *Multiple intelligences: The theory in practice.* New York: Basic Books.

Vygotsky, L.S. (1978*) Mind in society: The development of higher psychological processes.* Cambridge, MA: Harvard University Press.

FURTHER READING FURTHER READING **FURTHER READING** FURTHER READING

Brooks, V., Abbott, I. and Bills, L. (eds) (2007) *Preparing to teach in secondary schools: A student teacher's guide to professional issues in secondary education* (2nd edition). Maidenhead: OUP.

Capel, S., Leask, M. and Turner, T. (2001) *Learning to teach in the secondary school: A companion to school experience.* London: Routledge Falmer.

Ellis, V. (ed.) (2007*) Learning and teaching in secondary schools.* 3rd edition. Exeter: Learning Matters.

Petty, G. (2004) *Teaching today – A practical guide.* (3rd edition). Cheltenham: Nelson Thornes.

Useful websites

GTC Code of Conduct and Practice for Registered Teachers www.gtce.org.uk/standards/regulation/code_of_conduct/

Training and Development Agency for Schools (TDA): www.tda.gov.uk

Teachernet www.teachernet.gov.uk/

3
Beginning professional placement

By the end of this chapter you should:

- understand your professional responsibilities as a trainee teacher;
- be aware of the differences in school cultures and your place in the organisation;
- know what information you need to operate effectively within your placement school;
- know what data to gather in preparation for teaching your allocated classes, and where to source that data.

This chapter addresses the following Professional Standards for QTS:

Q3(a,b), Q4, Q13, Q30, Q32

Introduction

The purpose of this chapter is to introduce you to, and give you an overall view of, some of the key issues that you will need to embrace during your professional placement – but which you will need to be ready for and aware of at the beginning of your placement. Remember that these issues do not disappear once placement gets under way, but rather that this is what you need to know to make an effective start to each placement. Every school is different, and a successful start to placement can depend upon how well prepared for that experience a trainee teacher is.

Professional responsibilities

Perhaps the most important aspect of training to consider before you actually do anything is that of your professional responsibilities. You have already considered professional attributes in Chapter 1. The next stage is to understand what your professional responsibilities are – and who you are responsible to and responsible for.

PRACTICAL TASK PRACTICAL TASK PRACTICAL TASK PRACTICAL TASK PRACTICAL TASK

Think of all the people to whom and for whom you are responsible as a trainee teacher. Complete Table 3.1 in as much detail as you can to clarify these thoughts.

Table 3.1

Person responsible to/responsible for	Ways in which that responsibility is met
e.g. Responsible to a teacher whose class I have taken over	Keep up-to-date, accurate records of work and student progress

---

REFLECTIVE TASK
REFLECTIVE TASK

What is the difference between the people you are responsible to, and those you are responsible for? What is the difference in the impact on you, and on your perceptions of each person/group of people?

You have probably already realised that the Professional Standards for achieving QTS are all grouped under headings that begin with the word *professional*. Your attributes, knowledge and understanding and skills must all be developed within the framework of professionalism.

What you have on your list may differ from another trainee teacher's, but effectively there are particular things that are common to all professionals, and which it is absolutely crucial that you begin to develop. You need to understand your professional responsibilities in relation to the following people/groups.

The students

The people you are directly responsible for are the students in your care – for their safety and well-being while they are in your classroom. *Safety* does not only mean physical, it also means mental and emotional safety, and your classroom environment should support all of these. This element of your responsibilities links directly to the *Every Child Matters* agenda. It is also your responsibility to ensure that the classroom is an environment in which learning takes place; so you have responsibility for:

- monitoring the progress of your students;
- teaching and assessing all lessons which you have agreed with your subject mentor;
- ensuring that every child has the opportunity to learn to the best of their ability during every lesson.

This includes making sure that they have meaningful work to do even if you are absent from school for some reason, whether your absence is planned or not (e.g. a school trip, or you are ill). Make sure you have systems in place to do this, such as an email address for your mentor if it is an emergency, or a contact person to leave work with if the absence is planned.

You are responsible for students' pastoral care in your role as form tutor. The responsibilities concerning safety are exactly the same, but the role is slightly different. Here, you are often responsible for the more 'legal' aspects of the teacher's job: monitoring attendance, collecting absence notes and passing on information about planned absences such as doctor and dental appointments, and maintaining an overview of how your students are.

You are also responsible for your students when it comes to their general well-being. If you suspect that one of your students has special needs, has problems at home, is being bullied, or any other concern, it is your responsibility to follow this up. Make sure you learn the appropriate channels through which to do this; if you are unsure, find out before taking action.

The class teacher

You are responsible to the teacher of each class which you have taken over while you are on placement. If you are following an employment-based route, you may not have this responsibility, but your responsibilities towards the students are even greater because you are their class teacher. The professional responsibilities that come with this role are those related to:

- consulting about what the students are to be taught;
- recording what you have taught the students;
- returning students' work marked appropriately;
- returning recorded marks and assessment data.

The teacher will have to take over again when you leave, so they must be fully informed about what you have done with the students and what progress they have made.

Your subject mentor

You are responsible to your subject mentor in terms of fulfilling all of your professional responsibilities, as this person is effectively your line manager. It is very important that you comply with what your subject mentor asks for from you in relation to your training, such as lesson plans in advance, examples of marking to be discussed, schemes of work you are developing, and so on. You no doubt expect that they have responsibilities towards you – in turn, you must fulfil yours towards them.

Your head of department

You may be a guest in the department, but you must fulfil the professional responsibilities of all teachers towards their head of department, such as reporting of monitoring and assessment, following departmental procedures for sanctions and rewards, for attending departmental meetings, and for carrying out any roles that you are allocated within the department.

Your department team

It is your responsibility to become a colleague. Your responsibilities towards the department include respect for and adherence to its policies, taking care of its resources, acknowledging sources when you are supported and given resources or help, and also to share your own ideas, resources and expertise. The relationship is reciprocal, and you are as responsible for your place in the department as it is for welcoming you.

Your professional mentor

Your professional responsibilities here are similar to the ones you will have with members of the senior management team (SMT) when you are in post. You are responsible for ensuring that you attend the training sessions your professional mentor organises for you, that you respond promptly when they ask you to meet or for paperwork, and that you are clear about their role in your training, for example when they may observe you teaching.

The whole school

Whilst training, your relationship with the school is two-fold. Firstly, you are there as a trusted guest, aiming to become a colleague by the end of placement, and so you must uphold the ethos, values and policies of the school in which you have been placed. Secondly, you also have a responsibility to represent your ITTP well at the school in which you have been placed, and exemplify this in your own appearance, words and actions, whether you personally feel in sympathy with those values and policies or not. Your own success, and future placements of other trainees, depend upon this.

Parents

All parents must be treated with the utmost professionalism. This means that you do not judge them when you meet them, or use what you know about the student to colour your perception of them. No matter how parents speak to you, you must extend respect and manners to them at all times. Your responsibility here is to make the right judgement (with support from your subject mentor) about whether to call them, for what reasons, and what impact you anticipate the call may have on both the student and the parent.

Your visiting tutor

You may not realise it while you are training, but your visiting tutor has many commitments and so it is vital that you communicate with them when planned visits become disrupted by school life, which they often do. Make sure you arrange for your tutor to be met when they arrive at school, that the reception staff know that they are coming and what to do with them. Have all paperwork ready for presentation, and ensure that all files are up to date. This will make the visit run more smoothly, and leave only the lesson that is to be observed for you to think about.

Your ITTP

You have a responsibility to conform to the training requirements of your ITTP even though you are in a school which may do some things differently. So you must make sure that you are aware of what is required of you, for example using your ITTP's lesson-planning documents.

Your own training progress

No matter how much the school and your ITTP support you, ultimately you alone are responsible for your own progress. It is up to you to record evidence against the standards you must meet to gain qualified teacher status, to keep files up to date, to monitor your targets and work towards them, and to be open to criticism and advice.

As a professional, it is your responsibility to carry out all the duties of your post as a matter of course. It should always be possible to assume that you are doing so, and are ready for any call on those duties at any time, e.g. for checking that your marking is up to date because parents want to see their child's homework.

School cultures and 'fitting in'

The subjects on the curriculum may be the same in secondary schools and colleges, but the culture of every institution is different, and this is perhaps one of the most difficult aspects of your training to get to grips with. You will need to sound out the culture of each of your placement schools very carefully before you try to 'fit in' to it – and it may be a culture that you do not personally agree with. School culture is made up of so many factors that are almost indefinable: the area the school is situated in, the cultures and values of its students and their parents, of its staff, the ethos of the school in terms of sanctions and rewards, its role in the community, the style of the leadership of the school, and ultimately the individuals who make up the fabric of that institution. You will have to find a way to fit in with that culture, and although you must not do this at the expense of your own values, you need to learn to recognise when to speak up and when to support existing practices. So 'fitting in' might mean you have to challenge your own expectations of what a school is like as an institution.

REFLECTIVE TASK

REFLECTIVE TASK

Answer the following questions in as much detail as you can at several points during your training.

- At the very beginning of each phase of your training. This may mean in different schools, or at different points in the year in one school.

Moving on: at the end of your training.

- What kind of school culture do you want to work in?
- Why is this?
- What are your expectations of this school culture?
- What do you value about this kind of school culture?
- Why is this important to your working life?
- What will you gain from working in such an environment?
- What can you contribute to such an environment?

Keep your responses safe, and refer back to them each time you begin a new training phase and answer them again. They will give you a good idea of what it is that you perhaps implicitly find desirable in a school culture, but also of how your ideas change, if they do, as you gain experience of working in schools, which is an important reflection on your development as a teacher. The more experience you gain in school, the more your perceptions and expectations are likely to change.

Fitting in to the school culture may not be easy for you, especially if the type of school you are placed in is outside of your personal experience of education. You may feel like a fish out of water at the beginning of placement, but it is part of your professional responsibilities to respond appropriately to this and to make gradual changes that enable you to become part of the school, rather than stay as an outsider. If you are having problems with this, make sure you raise them with your subject mentor. However, you must do so in a way which is both professional and sensitive.

CASE STUDY
School cultures

Lucy was placed in an inner-city secondary school for her main placement. Her own educational background was in the public-school system, and for Lucy this comprehensive school was too far out of her own experience and she felt very uncomfortable there. She could not understand why the students did not want to learn, or why their parents did not make them do their homework. Lucy struggled with behaviour management because in her experience teachers were automatically respected, and she was not getting this herself. Her frustrations grew, and she began to talk to other members of staff, asking them why would they choose to work in a school like this; she couldn't understand how they got up in the morning to go to work. Lucy became very disheartened because she was not commanding respect and she could not relate to her students. Her classes were going very badly and the students were not making progress. Eventually Lucy's tutor came in and talked to her about the backgrounds of some of the students she was working with, and that although Lucy was working very hard to plan, it was not enough if the students did not sense that she was interested in them, and that they very quickly know if someone is not treating them with respect. Lucy listened very carefully to this advice and took it to heart, and began to get to know her students as people. She stopped expecting them to respect her and started listening to her students, and she found that her placement experience changed very quickly. She went on to successfully complete her placement.

School policies and systems

What are the policies and systems in this particular school, that enable it to function every day? You must get to know these before you begin each placement. Your serial days in school, if you have them, are the time to find out this information. Find out about policies for:

- behaviour (reward as well as discipline);
- the pastoral system including student absence;
- students with special educational needs, gifted and talented students;
- at-risk children;
- marking and assessment;
- equal opportunities;
- students with disabilities;
- organising trips.

Then you need to know what systems underpin these policies. You might know about the discipline policy, but do you know who to contact, how to contact them, and the full procedure for when you need to use it? Do you know how to report a child whom you suspect has a hearing problem? And so on. Make sure you know both the policy, and the system that supports it.

PRACTICAL TASK PRACTICAL TASK PRACTICAL TASK PRACTICAL TASK PRACTICAL TASK

Observe a daily routine in your department, focusing on how the day is supported by the policies and systems in place. Start with the morning briefing (if there is one) right through to the end of the day, including detentions, playground duties or extracurricular activities. Make a note of the following.

- Where a policy is referred to (this may be implicit – check with your mentor).
- What systems are followed, how, and by whom.
- What the outcomes of that policy and system are, where possible.
- Any times you suspect a policy is being followed, but you do not know what it is. Follow this up with your mentor at your weekly meeting.

Gathering and using school, national and student data

During the early days of your placement you will be getting to know your classes prior to taking over the teaching. One aspect of this is the use of data about your students. You will need to talk to your mentor about where and who you can get data from, and collect it as early as possible so as to inform your planning for your groups. There are several sources of data that you will need, as set out in Table 3.2.

Table 3.2

Student data	School data	National data
• Individual student marks/ levels from internal work done at school • Portfolio of evidence towards skill development (where available in school) • Informal reports from colleagues • Formal reports from previous reporting periods • Information from students	• MIDYIS (Middle Years Information System), YELLIS (Year Eleven Information System) and ALIS (Advanced Level Information System) tests • Information from school data manager – projected and predicted levels and grades • Departmental data	• From Year 6 SATs • Year 9 SATs • GCSE and GNVQ results • Fischer Family Trust data

Student data

Schools will record their own data about their students on a regular basis, so this will be the most up-to-date information you have. There may be levels or grades that have been submitted every half term that you can refer to, both in the subject you are teaching and across other subject areas, for comparison purposes. There will also be students' work that you can look at to see what their current targets are, what previous targets were and how the students have progressed. You can also ask the students themselves, of course, what they know about what they can and can't do – they are perhaps the richest source of data there is. You can locate this information through your subject mentor, the class teacher, and by looking at the students' work; for example, they may have a portfolio that they add to throughout the year. During the early stages of your training this is the data you may begin to look at first, and which you will contribute to most often.

School data

Schools generally make use of tests that are available to understand where their students are at by various points in their school careers. They may do these with tests such as MIDYIS, YELLIS and ALIS, which are externally designed and overseen by universities and are standard tests that provide a baseline for value-added measures of student achievement.

- MIDYIS: Years 7, 8 and 9
- YELLIS: Years 10 and 11
- ALIS: Post-16

These tests help schools to make comparisons between their own students and those in other comparable schools that take part in the projects. So a school can understand whether the progress their students are making is appropriate or not, based on similar students rather than the national picture painted by examinations. You can locate this information usually through your subject or professional mentor, or through the school's data manager if your school uses these tests. This may be an area to consider at later phases in your training, as will national data below.

National data

Some of this will come from the primary schools your students have attended, through the SATs (Standard Assessment Tests) that students take in Year 2 and Year 6, and you will also have the Year 9 SATs data to inform your work with students in Year 10 and Year 11. If you are working with post-16 students, you will also have GCSE and GNVQ results to draw upon. You can locate all nationally-derived data from the DCSF website (see Useful websites below).

REFLECTIVE TASK

Moving on

Gather data from as many different sources as you can about one of the classes that you are going to teach. Before you teach them, write a brief synopsis (500 words maximum) of your perceptions of the group in relation to the data. What do you think you will have to work on with this group? How are they achieving against predictions? What are the implications for you in terms of teaching and learning?

Return to this synopsis half-way through your placement. How accurate was the synopsis based purely on the data? Reflect on what you were able to put in place for this group as a result of the data analysis, and how the picture has changed since you have started to work with them. What do you now see as the role of the data in terms of beginning your placement?

Frequently asked questions

I have just found out that Year 9 reports are due in two weeks, and I don't feel I can meet the deadline, as the number of lessons I'm teaching is increasing each week.

You have a professional responsibility to deliver the reports on time – the school's reporting schedule cannot be held up for you. However, as you have only had two weeks' notice, you may want to talk to your mentor about this. Perhaps you and the class teacher can share the writing of the reports so that the task is achievable. Your first job is to communicate with your mentor so that they can help you to manage your workload. But the deadline in non-negotiable.

My professional mentor has asked me to do something that my subject mentor has said I don't have to do. I don't know what to do.

It depends on the context in which your professional mentor has asked you to do it, as it might be something as part of your whole-school training. It is worth clarifying this with your professional mentor, and the deadline for doing it. You may also mention this to your subject mentor, as it is part of your workload that they need to be aware of. This is not the same as complaining about it, though – make sure you do not do so! Such tensions are part and parcel of the teacher's workload.

The teacher of one of my classes does things differently to how my mentor does, and I resent them telling me so specifically what I ought to be doing when that is surely my subject mentor's role? How do I manage this situation?

Firstly, it is important to remember that if you have been given a class, you are to follow its teacher's lead about what to teach them. Your mentor oversees your training, but those classes remain the professional responsibility of their teacher, so it is very important that you follow their guidance about what you teach, when and how. However, you ought to be discussing these groups with your mentor as a matter of course, so you have an opportunity to discuss any issues you may have. Remember though that this must be conducted in a professional manner, and that the needs of the students are the most important consideration, not your needs as a trainee teacher.

A SUMMARY OF **KEY POINTS**

> Make sure you are fully aware of your professional roles and responsibilities. You must support and implement school policies, and understand how these impact upon school life on a daily basis.

> Speak to your mentor if you are having difficulty in meeting any of your professional responsibilities. You need to work together to find a solution that will enable you to fulfil those responsibilities.

> Spend time identifying the school culture before you behave as though you have always been there. Keep your tone in line with what you hear until you have established yourself more within the school.

> Speak to your subject and professional mentor if you are having difficulties with any elements of the school culture. Do this as soon as possible, when it is a small problem that can be solved.

> Gather data about the groups you will be teaching as soon as possible. Consider this carefully before you take over your groups so that you are pitching the work at an appropriate level when you begin.

REFERENCES REFERENCES **REFERENCES** REFERENCES **REFERENCES** REFERENCES

Arthur, J., Davison, J. and Moss, J. (1997) *Subject mentoring in the secondary school.* London: Routledge.

Dart, L. and Drake, P. (1996) Subject perspectives in mentoring. In D. McIntyre and H. Hagger, *Mentors in schools: Developing the teaching profession.* London: David Fulton.

FURTHER READING FURTHER READING **FURTHER READING** FURTHER READING

Brooks, V., Abbott, I. and Bills, L. (eds) (2007) *Preparing to teach in secondary schools: A student teacher's guide to professional issues in secondary education* (2nd edition). Maidenhead: OUP.

Useful websites

DCSF School and College Achievement and Attainment Tables www.dcsf.gov.uk/performancetables/
RAISEONLINE provides interactive analysis of school performance and data. You will need to access this from your placement school. www.raiseonline.org/login.aspx?ReturnUrl=%2findex.aspx
DfES (2003) *Every Child Matters* www.everychildmatters.gov.uk/publications
MIDYIS website: www.cemcentre.org/RenderPage.asp?LinkID=11410000
YELLIS website: www.cemcentre.org/RenderPage.asp?LinkID=11510000
ALIS website: www.cemcentre.org/RenderPage.asp?LinkID=11610000
Fischer Family Trust website: www.fischertrust.org/
GTC Code of Conduct and Practice for Registered Teachers www.gtce.org.uk/standards/regulation/code_of_conduct/

4
Planning and evaluating

By the end of this chapter you should:

- understand the importance of planning lessons/sequences of lessons;
- know how to identify learning objectives and be clear about what you want students to achieve by the end of the lesson;
- recognise the importance of planning starters and plenaries;
- understand planning for personalised learning;
- know how to plan homework and assessment opportunities;
- recognise the role evaluation plays.

This chapter addresses the following Professional Standards for QTS:

Q7, Q10, Q19, Q22, Q23, Q24, Q25(a–d), Q29

Introduction

The purpose of this chapter is to provide an overview of lesson planning and some key issues involved. Planning for learning is crucial to achieve student progress. It is vital to:

- plan teaching and students' learning carefully;
- learn from what happens as a result of planning and students' progress;
- use this evaluation to plan future learning.

Planning involves identification of learning objectives, lesson content and engaging resources, but considering other factors, for example, diversity of learners, variety of activity, student interaction, assessment, the time of day and preceding lesson helps lead to more successful lessons. If you have carefully planned a series of activities tailored to the abilities/needs/behaviour/interests of your students this will give you greater confidence in front of the class and help to avoid major difficulties.

Planning for learning: an overview

While on school placement you will be expected to produce a plan for *every* lesson you teach using the pro forma provided by your ITTP (or see exemplar in Appendix 1) and to evaluate each lesson (see Appendix 3) to demonstrate what you have learnt from your teaching and indicate how you can help learners make progress in future. You will use your department's schemes of work and policies to plan lessons and you may need to devise medium-term plans. These documents form your teaching placement file as a record of your thought processes and evidence of effective planning. Once your plan is produced, you will probably write notes and reminders on it or highlight certain sections, as it is a working document. As your career develops, carefully recorded evidence of planning and students' achievements will support your own professional development.

While a lesson plan is the tool you need to prepare for a successful lesson, lesson plans are not 'one-off' plans, but a constituent part of the continuum of students' learning. What happens in a lesson inevitably looks backwards to what students already know and have done, and forwards to what they will do next and in the longer term. Schemes of work reflect longer-term planning consisting of series of lesson plans, and demonstrate coverage of legislative and examination requirements, variety of methods and resources, assessment opportunities, etc.

This chapter will guide you through short-term planning and planning a lesson, identifying learning objectives, planning starters and plenaries, planning for personalised learning, medium-term planning, planning assessment opportunities and evaluating your lessons.

Short-term planning: planning lessons and sequences of lessons

When teaching a subject you have studied to a high level, your subject competence is clearly good, but as a teacher, you need to use that knowledge and transform it into something which is 'teachable' by you and therefore 'learnable' by your learners. You must:

- plan what exactly you want the students to learn (learning objectives) and what your learners will be able to do (learning outcomes);
- plan how you will enable them to do this (the manageable steps you will guide them through to achieve their aim);
- plan which resources you will exploit and produce to help learners acquire the required knowledge and skills.

Lesson planning involves a series of decisions made before, during and after the lesson. Activities need to be devised for presentation of the content and practice/application of understanding through a variety of tasks to maintain pace and interest. A successful lesson might look approximately as set out in Table 4.1 (though note that the point at which objectives are shared will depend on the class, circumstances and planned activities).

Table 4.1

Starter activity	(not token gesture but pedagogically valuable) plus register (if appropriate)
Objectives	(clear and useful, oral and written)
Activities	to 'get students learning' and address teaching points which: • are differentiated (matched) • focus on whole class/individual/pair/group as appropriate • consider the learner perspective • include clear and appropriate transitions and instructions
Assessment/evaluation	
Plenary	summaries/target setting/homework

The focus of any lesson/sequence of lessons should be the learners and their learning. What is the students' purpose: what will they learn in the lesson and longer term? How will they know how they're progressing? What do students know and what can they do already? What assumptions are you making? What do you want them to learn/be able to do? How will you know they can do this (during the lesson and afterwards)? Good lessons do not depend just on the amount of material prepared, but also on the ability of the teacher to motivate students and adapt resources well. In lesson plans topics need to be broken down to build on prior knowledge, develop concepts and processes and enable learners to apply new knowledge and skills.

Identifying learning objectives

Before planning a lesson it is important to identify your exact learning objectives. Consider your students' learning as a long journey. Before setting off you need to be clear where you are, decide exactly where you want to go and the most effective route for getting there. By outlining your objectives at the start of the lesson, students will have a clear idea of where they are heading and why and can be informed of their progress along the way to make the journey more fulfilling. Students will follow your instructions in lessons and do what you ask, but won't know the purpose of separate activities unless you explain. Objectives help students recognise the value of the work, and what they will have learned by the end of the lesson/series of lessons.

Objectives outline what you want students to learn during the lesson (not the tasks; for example, 'complete a worksheet' is not a learning objective.) Objectives need to be clear and realistic and indicate what students should achieve by the end of the lesson in terms of knowledge, understanding and skills. They need to be defined on the basis of prior learning outcomes to build on what students have learnt previously to consolidate or extend knowledge or apply skills in different contexts.

To cater for your students' different needs and abilities you may need to differentiate your objectives to personalise the learning and help to avoid lack of motivation:

- *all* students will . . . (must)
- *most* students will . . . (should)
- *some* students will . . . (could).

REFLECTIVE TASK

Consider this example of differentiated learning objectives for a history lesson. How could you differentiate learning objectives in your own subject?

Must understand that there are different interpretations of Cromwell's character

Should appreciate that interpretations of Cromwell have changed through the course of history

Could understand why interpretations have changed through the course of history.

REFLECTIVE TASK

From your school lesson observations, determine the learning objectives for each lesson. Did the activities enable students to achieve the learning objectives? Consider methods and processes during the lesson that led to success or hindered it.

PRACTICAL TASK PRACTICAL TASK PRACTICAL TASK PRACTICAL TASK PRACTICAL TASK

Now plan a lesson using either your standard planning pro forma, or the one that can be found in Appendix 1. Decide;

- *what* to teach;
- *how* to teach it;
- *which* activities/visuals/resources to use;
- *timing*;
- *order* in which to teach it all.

Follow the stages listed here to make it more manageable.

- Decide on the learning objectives.
- Plan your starter (a short activity to introduce the subject or a revision activity to practise prior learning or find out what students already understand).
- Introduce new content.
- Plan activities.
- Plan required resources.

Think about the following.

- What do you want the students to learn?
- How do you think they will learn it?
- What process will you use and why?
- How will you assess success?

Planning starters and plenaries

The Secondary National Strategy stresses the importance of a clear structure to lessons with starter, stimulating activities and plenary. Lesson starters:

- help to settle and focus students quickly;
- promote engagement and challenge;
- are active/collaborative;
- create an expectation that all students will participate and think.

Plenaries refocus students on the lesson objectives and give students a sense of achievement. Mini-plenaries may be used to check students' understanding and learning during the lesson as part of assessment for learning and therefore inform future planning. Plenaries provide a context for learning to relate the lesson's work to previous and future work. To conclude a lesson teachers could:

- take the students back to the objectives and forward to homework; and/or next lesson;
- check an activity conducted during the lesson, question students about it, assess their understanding informally and rectify any remaining misconceptions or errors;
- help students to draw conclusions, make rules, make links;
- ask students to evaluate their work; what did they learn, and how?

Variety in plenaries will prevent them from becoming meaningless mechanical activities.

BEELECLIAE 192K
REFLECTIVE TASK

Moving on

During later phases of your teaching, reflect on the use of the plenary and mini-plenaries during the lesson. What do you do at later stages in your training that you didn't do earlier? Why is this?

Planning personalised learning

As your school placement progresses, you will broaden your repertoire of teaching and behaviour-management strategies to match the needs of classes and individual learners. Knowing each learner's individual needs helps you plan differentiated learning objectives and activities so that all students are challenged to reach their potential.

While categorising different learning styles (visual, auditory, kinaesthetic) risks being too simplistic, it is important is to maximise your students' learning potential by providing variety of input and activity.

Planning for homework

Check school policies and plan homework (or 'home learning' as it is frequently called now) that is relevant to the learning objectives with achievable tasks appropriate to students' ability to sustain progress and consolidate learning. Consider at what point to set homework and plan a variety of homework types possibly with must/should/could tasks.

BEELECLIAE 192K
REFLECTIVE TASK

Think about the reasons why we set homework and the benefits to teaching and learning, and how the nature of the homework set changes in different year groups or key stages, and why.

Moving on

In later stages of your training, think about what you get from the homework you set, and how you use this. Do you set homework because school policy says you have to, or does it inform our assessment, planning and evaluations? How might you develop homeworks to become more useful to both you and your students?

Medium-term planning

An individual lesson plan is one of a series linking prior learning to future learning. Departments generally have schemes of work for each year group to act as a working handbook for teachers within the department. These should detail course content including progression and a broad timescale to work to.

Within the existing scheme of work you need to plan each class's work during school placement. Find out exactly at what point you will start to teach each class. To plan a series of lessons carry out the following procedures.

- Read through all available material: schemes of work, resources, teacher's plans, records. Scrutinise the topics, resources, teacher's notes, supplementary worksheets to grasp the whole chapter/topic. List all available resources.

- Determine the learning objectives (what the students should be able to understand/know/do).
- Determine what is reinforcement, core, extension material.
- List any opportunities for ICT, video/camcorder.
- Assessment opportunities: what is to be assessed and how? See Chapter 6 for more information about assessment.
- List appropriate homeworks.

Once complete, decide whether to use whole-class/pair/group work, or possibly carousel work. You can also decide whether to produce additional resources and whether there is chance for differentiation, guided and shared work or independent learning. Finally, think how it all fits into a 'diary' of lessons. Take each class one at a time. Set a few hours aside to consider everything mentioned above and how you will plan the lessons. Work varies for different levels of ability: for a lower set you need more basic work and reinforcement materials, for a higher set you need more extension work. Use the medium-term planning sheet exemplar in Appendix 2 to structure your planning.

Planning assessment opportunities

Assessment is integral to the planning, teaching and learning cycle (see Figure 4.1). It is not an end in itself, but is part of the ongoing cycle of teaching and learning.

Every lesson element from a single contribution to learning tasks, homework or course assignments, is assessed or evaluated to some extent. Teachers evaluate students' learning throughout lessons and at the end of lessons. From this informal assessment teachers often make intuitive judgements about the effects of their teaching and identify whether learners have grasped new knowledge or skills to determine what further practice/consolidation is required, how ready students are to move on and what feedback they require. Both formal and informal assessments evaluate and assess learning outcomes and assessment information is used to feed back to adjust planning where necessary.

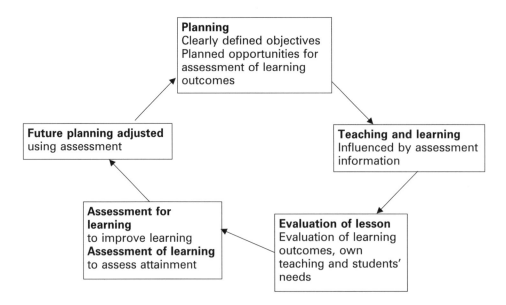

Figure 4.1. Planning, teaching and learning cycle

Planning assessment opportunities involves decisions about:

- *what* exactly is assessed;
- *when* assessment takes place;
- *why* assessment is conducted (measuring outcomes against objectives, planning ahead, diagnosing strengths and weaknesses);
- *how* assessment is conducted (individually/pairs/whole class, informally by observation or formally);
- *by whom* assessment is conducted (teacher, self, peers, a combination).

During planning, (whether short, medium or long term), you need to map assessment opportunities clearly. Informal assessment may develop overall judgements about class performance, including awareness that a particular student is not coping very well and that another seems to have made more rapid progress. However, this more informal feedback needs to be complemented by assessment of each individual. Teachers need to know how far individuals have met learning objectives, in order to provide assistance or guidance at an individual level, to feed back and therefore help learning to progress (assessment *for* learning) and to acquire a record of marks over a period of time (assessment *of* learning). Therefore, you need to think which activities could and should be assessed in each lesson (formatively/summatively); how you will assess them; how you can give instant feedback and targets by marking some work in class.

Assessment activities should be planned into the learning schedule, be chosen carefully, and have a specific focus or purpose clear to the learner. They should include a variety of task types designed to fit smoothly into the lesson and should allow learners a sense of satisfaction. Planning for formative assessment with feedback and targets to help improve progress should be a routine part of learning. It is important to choose the task types with which students are already familiar and which assess appropriate learning goals, while enabling students to perform at their highest level of ability. Chapter 6 will support you in doing this.

REFLECTIVE TASK

Investigate the school/ departmental policy on assessment. Now refer specifically to the work you are planning to teach during school placement. Reflect on how you will assess students' learning both during and at the end of this series of lessons.

PRACTICAL TASK PRACTICAL TASK PRACTICAL TASK PRACTICAL TASK PRACTICAL TASK

Devise opportunities for formative and summative assessment and add these to your medium-term plans.

Evaluation: your performance, students' learning, and the impact of evaluation on planning

The most important question to ask yourself after each lesson is: did the students meet the learning objectives, i.e. did the students learn what you intended them to learn?

Evaluating your lessons, and then series of lessons (to see how well learning objectives were met over the medium term), is crucial in monitoring and assessing students' learning. Assessment of students' learning occurs throughout the lesson, and in a more reflective way afterwards. This evaluation should inform your planning to build successfully on students' learning and skills and provide evidence for students' progress.

Careful evaluation is also important in relation to your development as a teacher. You will need to evaluate your own teaching and reflect on whether you need to modify your planning and classroom practice. You will evaluate your progress regularly against the standards and consider how to improve practice as each phase progresses.

Think about specific phases of the lesson. How successful were they? What factors led to the success or lack of it?

- The start.
- Transitions/activities.
- The end.

Did students understand the concepts?

Did the lesson build on preceding work for successful progression?

Was the lesson timed well or were sections rushed or extended unnecessarily?

Did you ensure maximum participation from all students?

How well did you use resources/materials? How appropriate were the resources you chose?

How did your differentiation strategies work? Did you support/stretch learners sufficiently?

Did the students learn what you wanted them to?

How would you evaluate the progress of individual students/groups of students?

Use the evaluation pro forma from your ITTP, or the one you can find in Appendix 3 after every lesson you teach, to inform and support your future planning, and at this stage in your career, to inform your own progress.

CASE STUDY
Moving on in planning
In her first school placement Victoria spent hours planning individual lessons. In spite of input from the university and her mentor she found it difficult to know where to start. But mid-way through her second placement she was able to see where each lesson fitted into a series of lessons, and this enabled her to plan a week's lessons in advance. She spent 10 to 15 minutes on planning each lesson and 45 minutes to resource the lesson (PowerPoint, worksheets, etc.).

REFLECTIVE TASK
REFLECTIVE TASK

Moving on

Compare your own progress with Victoria's. What strategies can you use to develop a longer term view and speed up individual lesson planning?

Frequently asked questions

I'm spending hours on planning. Does it always take this long?

Initially planning can be very time consuming. While planning is crucial, it is also important to be pragmatic, so setting yourself a time limit for each lesson plan may help. Plan during free time in school when all departmental resources are available and leave resource preparation for the evening when you are more tired. As your experience grows you will find that your planning speeds up. Seeing the bigger picture (medium-term planning) will assist the detail of each lesson.

How important is timing on plans?

Timing of individual activities is important although initially it can be difficult to judge this correctly. Trainees tend to plan too much for a lesson (or occasionally not enough.) Through observation and with experience, timing will improve and you will develop the confidence to adapt your plan to omit or follow through an activity effectively.

A SUMMARY OF **KEY POINTS**

> **Planning lessons and sequences of lessons is crucial for students' learning.**
> **The best plan involves clear identification of learning objectives and clarity about what you want students to achieve by the end of the lesson.**
> **Starters and plenaries structure the lesson.**
> **Each lesson needs to be adapted to match individual learners' needs.**
> **Appropriate homework reinforces and extends learning.**
> **Assessment is integral to the planning, teaching and learning cycle, opportunities for assessment must be planned.**
> **Evaluation plays a crucial role in monitoring your own performance and more importantly student learning.**

REFERENCES REFERENCES **REFERENCES** REFERENCES **REFERENCES** REFERENCES

Gardner, H. (1993) *Multiple intelligences: The theory in practice.* New York: Basic Books.

The Secondary National Strategy: www.standards.dfes.gov.uk/secondary/

FURTHER READING FURTHER READING **FURTHER READING** FURTHER READING

Elliott, P. (2007) Planning for learning. In Brooks, V., Abbott, I. and Bills, L. (eds) (2007) *Preparing to teach in secondary schools: A student teacher's guide to professional issues in secondary education* (2nd edition). Maidenhead: OUP.

Sotto, E. (2007) *When teaching becomes learning: a theory and practice of teaching* (2nd edition). London: Continuum International.

Useful websites

Teachernet www.teachernet.gov.uk/

The Standards website, provided by the DCSF, has exemplar schemes of work and lessons www.standards.dfes.gov.uk/

5
Teaching: delivering learning

By the end of this chapter you should:

- **know how to build a framework for developing learning in the classroom;**
- **understand ways in which you can draw on learning beyond the classroom;**
- **know how take your own development as a teacher forward by enhancing the learning of your students.**

This chapter addresses the following Professional Standards for QTS:

Q1, Q4, Q7(a), Q8, Q9, Q10, Q14, Q24

Introduction

The chapter is intended to signpost the development of the strategies you can use for developing learning through your teaching placements. Initially the focus is on developing the trainee teacher's skill in preparation and classroom communication. Once these aspects of the role are established, however, it is essential that the focus moves on to ways in which the teacher can involve students in their own learning and build motivation in this respect. Towards the end of the chapter we will be looking at some of the skills used by outstanding teachers to ensure progression in student learning and to foster the starting points for the students' lifelong commitment to their own development.

Making effective use of your teaching placements

This chapter is intended to help you to focus on the learning which takes place in your lessons whilst you are undertaking teaching placement. It is the role of the teacher to involve all students in learning and to ensure the best possible learning outcomes for those they teach. You must establish and develop your practice with this firmly in mind. The effectiveness of teaching is judged by the quality and extent of the learning which is delivered.

Getting started – the early weeks of teaching placement

Establish the starting points for learning

Use the initial stages of your teaching placements to find out about the prior knowledge and understanding of the students you will be teaching, taking into account what special students in your group (those with learning difficulties and with a high potential for learning) know and can do. Discussions with the class teacher and special educational needs co-ordinator (SENCo) will be relevant in this respect, but you should also refer to assessment records and test data. Your priority should therefore be to ensure that your lesson plans really do take learning forward from the starting points presented by your students when you take over the class.

Be clear about what you want to say

You are likely to be co-ordinating a number of activities and discussion sessions within each lesson, and initially you may find it difficult to deliver task instructions and teaching and learning sequences clearly. Before the lesson, it's useful to script key statements, task instructions and questions. Have your 'scripts' available in a readily accessible form (e.g. on the lesson plan – see Chapter 4) and refer to them just before you need the wordings concerned.

Subject your lesson plan to a 'reality check'

Consider the likely needs and likely behaviour patterns of various individuals in the group and work out where you may need to intervene to assist, or to get them on task. Once you have anticipated this, annotate your lesson plan accordingly. Reflect on what happened in the last lesson – was anyone away, in difficulty with their learning, or behind with home-work? Were any learning outcomes in doubt? If so, decide what you will need to do to pick up on these issues.

Think about potential misconceptions

As you build new learning, you will inevitably come upon common errors and misconceptions by your students. It is usually very helpful to consider in advance what these errors and misconceptions might be, and ways in which you can help to untangle ideas in this respect.

Develop good resource management techniques and classroom organisation

When you plan your lessons, you must also collect, develop or adjust the resources you will use to facilitate learning. Prior to the lesson itself, you will also need to decide how to manage these resources so that they can be provided for the students, and if necessary collected in, in ways which do not unduly delay, disrupt or curtail learning. You will also need to prioritise any safety issues.

REFLECTIVE TASK

Consider the following resource and classroom management requirements. What are the 'worst case scenarios' for disruptions in learning here? How can such disruptions be avoided by good resource management and classroom organisation?

- You want the class to copy a diagram from a textbook (the set of books is on your desk – there are enough for one between two) onto squared paper (also on your desk) using a pencil and ruler.
- You want the class to move into groups of four for the next task. You have already decided who should work with whom.
- Towards the end of the lesson you need to collect in a set of textbooks, a set of exercise books (the students have done some homework and you want them to leave their books open at the right page), a set of worksheets and 11 borrowed rulers.

Adapt your communication skills

As a teacher, you will need to trigger and shape learning through your verbal presentation. To achieve this, it is likely that you will need to develop your communication skills during the early stages of teaching placement. To do this you must keep the maturity of your audience firmly in mind and consider the full range of factors which are involved in teacher communication.

In the early stages of your training it is useful to observe other teachers and to note down effective features of communication.

As you develop your own teaching, ask for regular feedback from your mentor as you adjust your communication to the requirements of the teacher's role.

REFLECTIVE TASK
REFLECTIVE TASK

Rate yourself as a classroom communicator by giving a mark from 1 (weak) to 5 (excellent) for your use of the following communication skills.

- Gaining the interest of the class from the outset.
- Authoritative tone.
- Appropriate adjustment of tone.
- Volume.
- Appropriate adjustment of volume.
- Pace of delivery.
- Strategic use of pause.
- Appropriate selection of vocabulary and expression.
- Attention to teaching of vocabulary and expression.
- Immediate reinforcement through visual aids/media presentation.
- Appropriate length of teacher input.
- Effective checks for understanding of tasks and instructions.
- Body pose.
- Use of movement and gesture to convey meaning.
- Use of facial expression.
- Use of eye contact.

Ask your mentor to use this ratings system after an observation of one of your lessons and see how your views compare.

For any areas where improvement is necessary, set SMART targets 'specific, measurable, achievable, relevant, time-related' for short-term development.

Moving on

As you progress through your placement(s), undertake this reflective task at regular intervals. Consider how your practice is changing as your experience increases – and any areas where you are not making progress.

Moving on – generating student involvement in learning

Skilful teacher communication will help to provide a framework for the students' learning, but you must make sure that your commentary is limited to what is essential and that short teaching points are interspersed with individual or group tasks designed to promote learning.

Providing time for learning

Students usually like to be involved in tasks during the lesson, but you must ensure that the tasks you set have the capacity to take learning forward. You will need to consider the time spent on various tasks in your evaluation of the lesson, determining whether the time was well spent and whether learning could have been further enhanced in any way.

Review is an essential part of student learning (you should aim to spend approximately 20 per cent of learning time on review in various formats in order to consolidate learning), and you must therefore build time into your lessons for the review of learning.

Mixing commentary with questions

Try to make your explanations and reviews of learning tasks interactive by posing appropriate pre-planned questions. A good sequence of review questions will give you the opportunity to make connections in learning for students who have struggled, and to take forward the learning of others who have already made sound gains (see Chapter 6 for more strategies for questioning).

In many mixed-sex classrooms, adolescent girls are more reluctant to answer questions than boys. Supportive techniques should be of assistance in this respect, but remember that you can also pose questions to girls during group and individual working time as they may gain confidence in this less public setting.

Other opportunities for student involvement

Ensure that you also involve students in demonstrations, in presentations, in generating their own questions and in generally sharing their learning on a frequent basis to get a real 'team feel' to work and achievement in your classroom.

In Chapter 6 you will be reminded that students can also play a role in assessment work, particularly when this will enhance their learning in the lesson which follows. They can be involved in assessing their own work or that of others. Your aim as teacher should be to ensure that the students focus on positive points and that where there are weaker elements criticism is given in a sensitive and constructive manner.

REFLECTIVE TASK

Are there aspects of your teaching which could be improved to generate appropriate student involvement? If so, jot down personal targets under whichever of the following headings are relevant.

- Balance between teacher talk and student activity.

- Frequent use of appropriate questions.
- Pre-planning of questions.
- Broadening student response to questions.
- Allowing students to take the lead.
- Checking task instructions through student paraphrase.
- Involving students in critique.

Encouraging on-task learning behaviour

If students are going to develop their learning to the full in your lessons, they must remain on task during periods of individual or small group activity. The following recommendations may help you to build on-task learning behaviour.

- Develop seating plans for your group which prioritise learning relationships rather than social relationships.
- Pre-empt some difficulties by exploring typical errors and misconceptions before students begin their work.
- Act swiftly to put students who are likely to experience difficulty on the right track after work has begun.
- Use the teacher's desk as a work area for small groups of students who have common learning issues and who are likely to need your help on an ongoing basis.
- Improve the quality of learning during activity periods by providing students with worksheets which will help them to shape their learning and make progress.
- If discussion is appropriate, establish the desired noise level for the exercise, linking this to the learning to be achieved in your task instruction.
- Reduce the number of queries from students on more difficult tasks by setting up peer-group 'study buddies'.
- Ensure that your students are aware of the time constraints for each task and keep them appraised of the passage of time.
- Build in regular opportunities for checking how students are getting on with the task so that learning is not 'on hold' for significant periods of time.

PRACTICAL TASK PRACTICAL TASK PRACTICAL TASK PRACTICAL TASK PRACTICAL TASK

Ask your mentor, or another colleague, to observe one of your lessons and prepare a freehand graph showing on-task behaviour in relation to particular time points. Go on to link the time points to events and expectations within the lesson itself.

If off-task behaviour is a problem, go on to discuss ways in which this could be reduced by (a) your approach to the management of student learning, and (b) your approach to the management of student behaviour.

Moving on: progressing to teach outstanding lessons

As your training period progresses, you should aim to teach outstanding lessons. To do so you must have a thorough understanding of the particular ways in which teaching and learning strategies will enable students to make accelerated progress in your subject, and you must take an interest in innovative developments which could break new ground in these respects. Considerations from subject training, observations of leading practice in your subject, reading and reference to relevant websites and material from subject associations should all be drawn upon in consideration with your subject mentor, with a view to achieving sustained developments in your practice.

You may also wish to explore the following areas from a subject perspective.

The 'Learning Staircase'

You may well have been introduced to Bloom's taxonomy of learning domains (Bloom et al., 1956; see also Useful websites) in your training course. This suggests that our ability to use our learning develops through the stages illustrated in Figure 5.1.

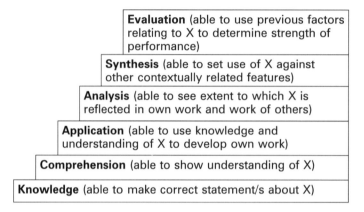

Figure 5.1. The Learning Staircase

Each area of the curriculum has its own contextual interpretation of the higher thinking skills on this staircase.

REFLECTIVE TASK
REFLECTIVE TASK

Consider what would be involved in a structure of this type for your own teaching subject. Discuss this with your school mentor.

If you are going to ensure that learning in your subject moves beyond the lower steps of the learning staircase, you will need to consider how you can build students' awareness at levels which show a higher level of capability. You may wish to explore the following possibilities.

- Base your learning objectives and activities on a step-by-step learning progression through a range of levels on the learning staircase.
- Work through levels of Bloom's taxonomy when planning question sequences.
- Find appropriate opportunities to use sequences of questions which reflect the taxonomy to the whole class, to a specific group of students or to individuals.

Thinking of learning in this way can be daunting, but if you engage in team planning with your mentor and consider outcomes together, this should make you feel more secure. You will probably need a month or so to embed these techniques, but after a deliberate focus period you'll find that reference to progression in learning in your subject will become a habit in your preparation and teaching of lessons.

Enhancing learning through your lesson structure

Chapter 4 looked at effective ways of structuring a lesson through the presentation of clear learning objectives, activities which are directly relevant to these objectives, and review/plenary feedback focussed on the learning which has taken place. As your teaching develops, and particularly as you move into later phases of your training, you will need to ensure that you are making the best possible use of these elements in order to deliver learning. Furthermore, your students will need to be made aware of the learning plan which underpins your lesson structures and schemes of work if they are to apply their efforts appropriately and collaborate in taking their own learning forward.

REFLECTIVE TASK

Moving on

Questions which you might ask as part of your lesson evaluation are as follows.

- Were the learning objectives clear, in 'student speak', and was essential technical vocabulary explained?
- Did I check that the students understood the objectives?
- Did I clarify how achievement of the learning objectives would help the students to progress?
- Were the learning outcomes differentiated to offer an appropriate learning challenge for all students?
- Did I demonstrate the link between student activities and the learning objectives effectively?
- Did my question sequences support appropriate learning outcomes?
- Did my reviews and plenary engage students in reflecting on the extent to which the learning objectives had been achieved?
- Did I 'signpost' future learning – i.e. show how the students will be taking today's learning further in the remaining sessions of the unit or scheme of work?

Making the most of your final plenary session

The plenary session at the end of your lesson offers students a very important chance to review their learning and to see if they can apply it in different circumstances. Planning an effective plenary is quite an advanced skill and one which you should spend time on with your mentor and with others in school in order to develop an effective range of approaches. You may wish to do a range of mini-observations, getting an agreement to join colleagues during the last 15 minutes of their session so that they can model the use of a well-designed plenary for you.

CASE STUDY

The science team has a scheme of work on calories as energy. In one of the lessons within this scheme students bring in small pieces of food of various types and burn them over a Bunsen burner to see which burns for longer and hence contains more units of energy. The teachers use a variety of plenary structures in this lesson, based on the needs of their students. The plenary structures they employ are as follows.

Ask students to demonstrate their learning by writing definitions of the key words for lesson on their mini-whiteboards and discussing strong suggestions. Ask why understanding of each key word is important. Link the key words back to relevant learning objectives and discuss with students where they feel secure learning has taken place, and where further reinforcement will be needed in the next lesson.

Ask students to consider how the word 'energy' has been used in the context of the lesson and to show a definition on their mini-whiteboard. Establish appropriate/agreed definition. Ask what we usually mean by 'energy'? Students to show this on reverse side of their whiteboard. Establish agreement in this respect. Provide a list of five snack foods with their calorie count. What exercise and exercise duration would you recommend to help the body burn up calories provided by the snack foods listed? Discuss student views.

Nominate students as Person A and Person B in their pairings. All students nominated as Person A should write down three conclusions which they have been able to make about foods, calories and energy from the burning experiment. All students nominated as Person B should write down three conclusions which they have been able to make about safety in science experiments. Students should then share ideas with their partner. Ask student pairs to identify which learning objectives their conclusions relate to. Ask six students to contribute by each giving one of their conclusions and relating this to the relevant learning objective.

REFLECTIVE TASK
REFLECTIVE TASK

Moving on

Consider the plenary structures above used by members of the science team and make a note of their relative merits. Which learning needs would each plenary address? How might you change the plenary you would use, and why?

Engagement techniques

If students are to gain a really good grasp of what you are teaching them, you must extend the 'learning moment' when the focus is on acquiring new knowledge and skills so that key aspects are fully understood. Approaches which extend the learning moment are called engagement techniques. Extend your awareness of a range of engagement strategies for your subject through reading – Unit 11 on 'Active Engagement Techniques' within the *Pedagogy and practice: Teaching and learning in secondary schools* (series 2) is particularly helpful in this respect, and through discussion with your subject mentor. Begin to use those engagement techniques that seem more appropriate, and begin to adapt others by thinking through possible uses in the context of your subject.

PRACTICAL TASK PRACTICAL TASK PRACTICAL TASK PRACTICAL TASK PRACTICAL TASK

The list below contains a number of engagement techniques.

Text marking

Improvisation

Segmenting – students divide text into labelling sections

Card sort – sequencing activity

Make a table (presenting given information in tabular form)

Students collaborate with one another in writing

Odd one out

Maps or diagrams from memory

Hot seating

Concept mapping

Interpreting pictures

Demonstration of concepts through student movement or freeze frame

Making predictions

Students prepare list of questions

Speculative questioning (repeated 'what ifs...')

Use this list as the beginning of an *aide-mémoire*, and add other ideas to widen the range of options.

REFLECTIVE TASK

Which engagement techniques could you usefully adapt to build up new approaches to learning in your lessons? Mark these with a tick and make notes as to how you intend to develop these ideas to take learning forward.

Flexible control of pace and timing

As your teaching skills and awareness develop, you should find it possible to adjust the pace of activities, perhaps drawing out question-and-answer sessions where learning seems particularly fertile and compensating by shortening a group or individual learning task. In your planning, you should decide how to create extra time for key learning moments. You may find the following suggestions helpful.

- Reduce the time spent on exploration tasks by setting different starting points and allowing ground to be covered by the students corporately, rather than by individuals or groups.
- Build in an exercise in which points are prioritised before asking for discussion feedback.
- Give half of the class one task, and half another (rather than expecting students to work through both tasks), and then ask for feedback on content and learning.

You can also improve differentiation for students who are achieving at different levels by strategically varying the pace of work for different groups. For example, lower achievers can work at a reinforcement pace, broadening their awareness through different applications, whilst higher achievers are set on a shortened course through classwork so that they can move on to extension exercises with time to develop new learning.

> **PRACTICAL TASK** PRACTICAL TASK PRACTICAL TASK PRACTICAL TASK PRACTICAL TASK
>
> Begin to work on the flexible use of pace with your subject mentor or with another strong teacher in your department. Talk about ways in which pace can be adjusted in your subject. Look at the planned learning coverage of your colleague for given lessons with Year 7, Year 9 and Year 11. Observe the lessons.
>
> ● How is good learning pace achieved with each year group?
>
> ● Can you see where pace is being deliberately adjusted to meet the learning needs of the group?
>
> ● Is the teacher encouraging students to move through their work at a varying pace? Are there points where this could be achieved?

Creating opportunties to learn beyond the classroom

In school we tend to think of learning as being relevant to the qualifications framework. The idea of developing the students' lifelong capacity for learning is a much stronger motivation, however, and part of your role as a trainee teacher will be to begin to open up the learning environment so that students have the knowledge and skills they need to voluntarily take their studies further beyond the classroom. For homework, provide your students with well thought-out 'knowledge quests' and investigative opportunities and you will find them bringing back vital contextual knowledge for in-school projects, as well as a growing appetite for learning in your subject.

A SUMMARY OF **KEY POINTS**

> During your teaching placements your focus on learning, and the positive learning outcomes which students can achieve, should steadily increase.

> Ensure that you are aware of your students' starting points in terms of prior knowledge and understanding and learning needs.

> Plan the organisation of your lessons very carefully so that nothing impedes learning.

> Spend time in the early stages of your practice developing communication skills for teaching.

> Use strategies which encourage students to become more involved in their own learning.

> Be prepared to work in ways which develop the students' learning capability.

> Use the potential offered by lesson structure to maximise learning and the awareness of learning.

> Ensure that you are using a range of active engagement techniques to focus student learning in your subject.

> Adapt the pace of lesson activities to create more scope for learning, for the class as a whole or for specific groups.

> Encourage students to continue their learning beyond the classroom.

REFERENCES REFERENCES **REFERENCES** REFERENCES **REFERENCES** REFERENCES
Bloom, B.S., Ebgelhart, M., Furst, E., Hill, W. and Krathwohl, D. (1956) *Taxonomy of educational objectives: The classification of educational goals, Handbook 1: Cognitive Domain*. New York: Longmans Green.

Pedagogy and practice: Teaching and learning in secondary schools, DfES 2004 (a range of 20 booklets on aspects of teaching and learning, together with related DVD material). Booklets can be downloaded from the Standards site – www.standards.dfes.gov, and related DVD material can be provided through Teachers TV – www.teachers.tv.

FURTHER READING FURTHER READING **FURTHER READING** FURTHER READING

Ellis, V. (ed.) (2007) *Learning and teaching in secondary schools* (3rd edition). Exeter: Learning Matters.

Useful websites

Materials related to subject teaching within the Teacher Training Resource Bank www.ttrb.ac.uk

For a detailed and helpful look at Bloom's taxonomy, look at the University of Victoria's website: www.coun.uvic.ca/learning/exams/blooms-taxonomy.html

6
Assessment, monitoring and reporting

By the end of this chapter you should:

- understand the role and impact of assessment on teaching and learning today;
- know the differences between formative and summative assessment;
- be familiar with the basic principles of assessment for learning;
- understand the personalised learning agenda and how it relates to assessment in the classroom;
- be able to recognise the importance of reporting and feedback to a range of audiences, considering, in particular, purpose and possible content.

This chapter addresses the following Professional Standards for QTS:
Q11, Q12, Q13, Q26(a), Q27, Q28

Introduction

This chapter is designed to prepare you in confidently getting to grips with assessment requirements during your school placement, which include the monitoring and reporting of students' progress and their achievements.

During your training, assessment is often introduced as a discrete feature within the curriculum. Although this is understandable when working with a range of targeted standards, it is important that you learn to recognise and value assessment as an integral feature of all your teaching and learning. It would be a misunderstanding to think of assessment as an end game, a bolt-on or an adjunct to your teaching. The process of recognising progress and achievement is an 'active' ingredient in the planning and delivery of each lesson.

In recent years assessment has been experiencing a renaissance, with an emphasis on its formative qualities, rather than the traditional focus on summative judgement. Formative assessments are made at regular intervals in a scheme of work or assessment period and are designed to offer clear feedback to learners on what they can do to improve their performance prior to a summative assessment being made. Summative assessments are often the final and recorded grade or level given at the end of a scheme of work or period of assessment; exams, SATS, end-of-year tests, etc., are all examples of summative assessment.

Making and assessing progress

The QCA (Qualifications and Curriculum Authority) (2008a) has recently introduced *A fresh approach to assessment*. This initiative explores ways of recognising evidence of learning and in particular different ways of looking or more essentially seeing what learners do and say and responding actively to this. There are three key features or ways of recognising evidence of learning and which should focus your own approach to assessment, monitoring and recording whilst on placement. These are:

- close up;
- standing back;
- public view.

The first is about looking and listening 'close up', which recognises and responds to the 'day-to-day' understanding of assessment. You should understand this as immediate feedback, with a view to adjusting your short-term planning to meet students' needs.

The second feature is 'standing back', a form of periodic assessment which enables both teacher and learner to reflect on the overall performance of a scheme of work or particular feature of the learning. This is designed essentially to inform medium-term planning, recognising and responding to individual strengths and needs, with a view to personalising learning.

The third and final feature is the 'public view', which in most instances determines a student's next steps in learning and in their lives.

At the heart of this approach is a focus on assessing pupils' progress (APP), equipping teachers to make informed judgements about those they teach (QCA, 2008b). It is about recognising and responding to individual needs such that students can become partners in the art and science of teaching and learning, with a view to ensuring progress and achievement. You will find out more about the theory of APP and the new approach to assessment from your ITTP, and from your placement school(s) about how they put these into practice.

Actively engaging with assessment

Schools are now prioritising assessment for learning as an equal, if not senior partner in what has been historically understood as assessment of learning. So what is the difference in practice? In brief, assessment for learning is a process that enables teachers and students to identify where the individual is at in their learning, where they need to get to next and what action should be taken in order to achieve this. Assessment for learning therefore needs to exist at the heart of the planning process. It also requires a high level of transparency, ensuring that students are actively engaged in the assessment process and not simply passive recipients of it.

Young people in today's classrooms are expected to aim high. Like you, they recognise and are working towards a set of standards in everything they do. It is recognised by teachers that if students choose to, and are motivated by good and responsive teaching, they can both meet and often exceed expectations. It is with this in mind that we begin to see the potential role that assessment for learning can play in educational reform; for example, its capacity to improve your teaching and learning approaches, whilst positively impacting on the social health and development of your class. And like evaluation, effective assessment and monitoring are crucial in enabling you to plan future lessons that meet the needs of your particular students. Thus there are significant implications for your development as a trainee teacher in relation to developing your assessment strategies and practices.

Beginning assessment

As with all aspects of your training, meeting the standards in assessment, monitoring and reporting is a progressive experience that spans your school placement(s). Although you may well be confident with the features of assessment as a theoretical concept, what is imperative is that you are able to make sense of this in practice and over time. So where does practice begin? Table 6.1 is a needs analysis chart which could act as a simple guide for your introduction to and development in assessing, monitoring and reporting pupil progress. During your time on placement there should be three phases towards competency in this field.

1. Observation and enquiry, which allows you build a bigger picture of assessment within the school.
2. As you work towards securing your ability to plan for and structure learning, there will be a need for sourcing data on those students you are now responsible for.
3. As your practice develops you will find yourself with increasing responsibility for handling, and more importantly, producing assessment data to inform and personalise learning for your students.

PRACTICAL TASK PRACTICAL TASK PRACTICAL TASK PRACTICAL TASK PRACTICAL TASK

Use the following needs analysis chart at regular intervals during placement, including at the beginning of every new placement, as a guide to recognising and acting on development in this field. This could form the basis of regular discussion with your mentors in school, especially as your experience increases.

Table 6.1

Needs analysis during placement	Emergent, established or revisiting
Am I familiar with department policy on assessment? *How does this compare with whole-school policy for assessment?*	
Do I understand how the school recognises achievement and what initiatives it employs to monitor and report this back to pupils, staff, parents and governors?	
Am I clear about the whole-school approach to assessment and how this compares with what is happening at a departmental level? *What are the school/department strengths in this field? What new initiatives are being introduced? What impact are these having?*	
Have I met with the assessment co-ordinator and or data manager for the school? *What kinds of data are available for teachers to use? What data is available for the classes I will be teaching?*	
Have I clarified what expectations the department has regarding the assessment of my students from the beginning of placement? *Do I understand how, when and what to assess during my teaching placement?*	
Do I have evidence of assessment becoming 'active' in my short- and medium-term planning, through learning objectives, differentiation, success criteria, assessment strategies, formative and summative?	
Can I talk confidently about the range of formative assessment strategies I have used in my teaching and learning and the impact that this is having? *Does my planning show evidence of this?*	
Can I provide a record of assessment outcomes over a period of time and through a range of learning opportunities for each of the classes I teach?	
Have I used these records to set actionable targets against students' work?	
Do I have assessment data for each of the classes that I teach?	
Am I able to use assessment data to inform such things as planning, report writing, parents' evenings, homework activities, preparation for examinations?	

Once in school you will find that it is almost impossible to separate assessment from the curriculum, as it is the content of this that informs what an individual should know, understand, be able to do, as well as providing the context for how and when this measurement of 'quality' and/or 'ability' should take place. So as soon as you know what your classes are studying, you will be able to match this with a set of given assessment criteria and/or objectives.

Remember at all times during your placement you are looking to make connections with curriculum content, learning objectives, learning and teaching styles, assessment criteria and therefore assessment strategies, both formative and summative. You are looking back on prior learning, at current knowledge, and what this is leading towards, and matching your assessments to the most appropriate learning and teaching styles to help students' progress. So your process will consider all of the following.

- **Generic objective**. Prescribed by the National Curriculum or examining body.
- **Contextual objective**. Personalised for the class and individual needs.
- **Assessment opportunities**. Identified assessment points in short-, medium- and longer-term planning.
- **Assessment criteria**. Evidence of achievement.
- **Strategies and/or means of assessment**. Selected to ensure a range of achievements in a diversity of contexts.

Moving on: strategies for effective formative assessment in classroom practice

As your placement develops, you will become aware that assessment for learning is happening all around you: during lessons, outside of lessons, informally, formally; that it is being led by both teachers and pupils, in silence or during a whole-class debate. It can happen in role as a Viking or music producer, in the school hall or on a field trip. Assessment for learning is a living and breathing tool designed to help individuals make sense of where they are in their learning, whilst giving them the confidence in knowing how to move on or, better still, providing them with the impetus to want to move on. However, in order for this to happen by design rather than by accident it relies on you getting the pedagogy right, and so this is something for you to consider as you gain experience. Below is a series of pedagogical strategies that focus on producing knowledge, not re-producing it. All of the examples are focused on teaching towards real and relevant assessment tasks.

Rich questioning

Most lessons will include questions from the teacher and responses from the students; however, what is often more difficult to ensure is a lesson in which there is evidence that questions have been thoughtfully premeditated during the planning process in order to generate new learning. Being able to prompt a range of rich or insightful responses that provide a high degree of challenge questions needs careful consideration. For understandable reasons of time and coverage, teachers often look for instant responses as a means of confirming a superficial level of subject knowledge and legitimising the move to the next task. Bloom's taxonomy (which you were introduced to in Chapter 5) suggested that there is a hierarchy of thinking skills – knowledge, comprehension, application, analysis, synthesis, evaluation. It is with this in mind that we turn our attention to the 'richness' of a question, one which does not simply test memory or seek a single correct answer, but rather requires students to experience and engage with increasingly higher-level skills in the hierarchy, and in particular the three highest-level skills – analysis, synthesis and evaluation.

Questioning in action

Questions could be planned in advance and differentiated to ensure that students are encouraged to analyse and synthesise information from different perspectives. This will also mean that they begin to evaluate the findings from ethical and social as well as academic criteria. Consider how to structure questions which build on from initial student response. If you are interested in the answers you'll ask a more interesting question.

Thinking time

The thoughtful process of engaging with a given question should be valued over vocal responses that are often immediate and unsubstantiated. The 'no-hands' strategy is a valuable technique for engaging all pupils in questions, whilst allowing or requiring that time is given to 'think' through possible responses. All contributions should be valued and developed, however small or uncertain they might at first appear. Target and name pupils and invite them to give a response and build on their responses with further questions or praise.

Thinking time in action

Responses could be fed back to a partner, written down in books or on mini-whiteboards and held up or fed onto a large sheet for everyone to read. You might also encourage students to make diagrams or other kinds of graphic 'doodling' if this helps them to think.

Rich activities

As with a rich question, a rich activity is something which should appear to students as an alluring problem or challenge that demands an imaginative and or creative response. It should at the same time encourage access, albeit at different entry levels, from all students regardless of ability. It should also provide students with a context for learning which is intriguing, inspiring the need for dialogue and collaboration, and prompting ideas that encourage originality through speculation, negotiation, analysis and reflection. Usually, rich activities will look like real world activities – jobs and projects that are authentic and like the work that people actually do.

Rich activities in action

When designing your rich activity, ask yourself: does it enable you to assess what your students already know; is there sufficient challenge so you identify what support they will need to reach new depths in their learning; are there sufficient stages in the activities to challenge the most able and motivate the least? Will it lead you to think about what learners will need to know next?

Dialogue

This means sustained conversation and discussion between teacher and student, or student and student. It is through dialogue that the learner can be encouraged to re-question, enquire, exchange or challenge ideas, and perhaps crucially be given the opportunity to view a response from a variety of perspectives and therefore potentially make new meaning. It has been shown that opportunities for sustained conversation between learners as well as with the teacher are crucial to successful learning (Newmann et al., 1996).

Dialogue in action

When planning a lesson ensure that there is opportunity for students to engage in structured and meaningful dialogue over question and response. The more you listen, the more you can learn about your students and how best to help them.

Focusing feedback/feedforward

Feedback or feedforward, written or verbal, given by the teacher or in a peer-led situation, are vital if the learner is to understand where they are currently in their learning and what they need to do in order to move forward. Receiving a grade or a level will position you in terms of achievement, but it does little to identify your strengths or more importantly, how you can improve. Regular, positive, aspirational and realistic feedback in different forms is at the centre of the idea of personalised learning. It ensures that each student is in constant dialogue about his or her own distinctive performance and needs. Feedback/feedforward can range from the quick and informal chat in the corridor to a sit-down meeting with a formal record. Assessment without feedback/feedforward can result in a decline in performance and/or a lack of interest in actually wanting to improve.

Feedback/feedforward in action

When target-setting, ensure that targets are made 'actionable'. Students need to be able to act on feedback. Ensure that what is spoken or written is either interpretive or evaluative, outlining what has been achieved and how the work could be improved. Ensure also that for every area of improvement there are at least two aspects of the work that identify a success or strength. This balance is important in motivating the individual, knowing that they are making progress but also that there is still room to improve. It is also worth noting that if you are working with given criteria for assessing the task or work, you should use this to frame your responses.

Negotiating targets

It might seem a simple act, but involving students in their own targeting-setting is the difference between encouraging passivity and compliance or responsibility and engagement, whereby learners are able to demonstrate independence and can begin to connect confidently with their own learning. The act of negotiation or reaching an agreement can only be achieved through dialogue, in which an individual is required to respond and as a result becomes involved in the target-setting process.

Negotiating targets in action

Finding the time to negotiate targets might appear like a time-consuming activity. However, these negotiations might begin with peer dialogue. Your targets could become the focus of their negotiation.

Self and peer assessment

The idea of self and peer assessment allows the learner to become an active participant in the assessment process, resulting in the desire and/or need to understand the assessment process and the associated vocabulary. Rather than the teacher always being central to or determining the progress of an individual, this emphasis begins to shift, with the student over time taking ownership of his or her learning. With this comes a greater sense of self-awareness and a growing urgency to self-monitor, identify and engage in a dialogue with their teacher and/or peers about their own learning and strategies for progression.

Self and peer assessment in action

Ensure that any self and/or peer assessment is guided by a set of criteria, whether these be decided by you and your class, or nationally agreed. All learners need dialogue framing to ensure that 'talk' and 'feedback/forward' are purposeful and actionable.

CASE STUDY

Although Jaspreet was making satisfactory progress on her placement in summative assessment, it had been observed that she was struggling to understand assessment as an active and integrated feature of her lesson. Her own experience of assessment at school always involved working under test-like conditions, in silence, independently and often with a time constraint. She felt that this had done her no harm and more than anything enabled her to clearly identify what students had learnt at regular intervals. Feedback was always graded, providing her with a sense of confidence, knowing that she could keep a regular record of individual achievement. A brief comment on the quality of the work always accompanied the grade, but there was little evidence of actionable targets being set. In response to this her subject mentor invited her to observe a number of different colleagues in the faculty using assessment for learning strategies as the preferred style of monitoring and assessing progress. It was from this experience that she began to make connections with students becoming partners in the assessment process and more importantly taking ownership of their learning. During the lessons she was encouraged to make an audit of AFL strategies used and consider the advantages of each one. What she began to discover was that the teachers embedded assessment within the teaching and learning process. This allowed for immediate feedback on student progress, with targets for improvement being negotiated during the lesson. It was agreed that Jaspreet would begin by planning for one active AFL strategy to be used in each lesson and to reflect on this through her evaluation.

PRACTICAL TASK PRACTICAL TASK PRACTICAL TASK PRACTICAL TASK PRACTICAL TASK

Identify within your department the range and/or types of tasks that pupils are being assessed through, e.g. written, research, performance. You may find this through discussion, observation or through departmental handbooks.

REFLECTIVE TASK

What signals are being sent to students across the school by the type of work they are being assessed through? For example, are they assessed mostly on their written work?

PRACTICAL TASK PRACTICAL TASK PRACTICAL TASK PRACTICAL TASK PRACTICAL TASK

Moving on

List the range of assessment for learning strategies that are used within a) your department, b) across the school. How do these compare? Go on to consider at what point in the students' learning a particular strategy is used and why.

Monitoring student progress

Improved standards at a local or national level are determined by the quality of teaching and learning that take place in the classroom. Therefore when we start to think about how this is monitored we should begin to recognise ourselves 'within' this process rather than as a target of it. Monitoring does not need to determine our classroom practice, but it should draw our attention to learning in partnership. Where there is a need for monitoring, there will always be that which is or those who are monitored. Accountability is synonymous with the teaching profession and therefore there is a genuine need for monitoring, ensuring consistency and continuity for both teachers and learners, knowing that what is said to be happening matches the reality. We are accountable not only to those we teach, but to the parents or carers of those we teach, to those who have employed us or are providing us with a place to train, to the governing bodies who drive school change and to those external agents who measure progress and achievement locally against a national framework. How we teach, what we teach and the values that are placed on assessing this should be made transparent for all.

Making reporting matter

Reporting in school can take many different appearances for a range of audiences and occasions. During your placement you will find that you are accountable, not only to the students in your care, but also to their, parents, class teachers, examining bodies and other members of the school/community. Therefore it is important that you begin to consider the different people you might find yourself reporting to and, equally important, the mode, method and manner in which you will do this. Report writing is another extension of school 'partnership', both inside and beyond the classroom environment. Your students should also be encouraged to keep formal and informal records of their own progress and attainment. Increasingly these student recordings will be kept as e-portfolios and available for access at regular intervals. Any comment, spoken or written should be personal, meaningful and time-efficient.

- **Personal**: Do you know who this learner really is? Do your records give a personalised picture of progress?
- **Meaningful**: In what ways are your records consequential to the learner? Are you aware of their previous targets? Can you identify their strengths? Could give an example of a recent achievement? What have you negotiated in terms of new targets? How are these been monitored? What support is in place to ensure s/he meets them?
- **Time-efficient**: Is this recording happening at a regular time? Do you have one place in which you record all assessment-related activity?

PRACTICAL TASK PRACTICAL TASK **PRACTICAL TASK** PRACTICAL TASK **PRACTICAL TASK**

Using Table 6.2 begin to map out the range of occasions where you might find yourself in an informal and/or formal setting giving feedback and/or reporting during your current placement. Consider the headings in at least three different situations which require both oral and written types of reporting.

Table 6.2

Reporting	Oral	Written
Purpose?		
When?		
Language?		
Content?		
Advantages?		
Potential pitfalls?		
Record of evidence?		

REFLECTIVE TASK

What has this task revealed to you about feedback and reporting in your school's setting?

Frequently asked questions

My subject mentor has said that I need to provide evidence of how I am monitoring student progress. What strategies could I use to do this?

You need to consider beginning by identifying the range of methods available to you. Talk to your subject or professional mentor about these and then begin to separate the formal methods from the informal, for example student feedback versus collecting samples of students' work or the analysis of test data over classroom observation. You should also consider the time that each of these methodologies might involve for example an informal exchange between other members of staff could take place during break time. Alternatively, you might choose quantitative data over qualitative for example measuring your students' grades against local or national comparative data. Does one method have an advantage over another? Which do you think might be most be most effective given your circumstances?

Do I need to make a written record of assessment during and after each lesson?

You should ensure that there is an activity within each lesson that enables you to make an assessment of students' progress to inform future planning. Whether or not this assessment is formal and recorded or not will depend on context. Your students should also be involved in recording assessment outcomes, with a view in particular to self and peer assessment opportunities. In addition to this you might choose to keep an assessment notebook for each class, which records observations you make on whole-class and individual progression. Not only will this support the monitoring process, but it will develop your strength and confidence in reflective practice.

A SUMMARY OF **KEY POINTS**

> **Know that how we learn becomes what we learn.**

> **Assess and value the process of learning as well as the product and outcome.**

> **Use assessment to motivate and reward; agree attainable targets.**

> **Students should be actively involved in aspects of assessment.**

> **All assessment, summative or formative, should be used to help young people move forward in their learning and in their lives.**

REFERENCES REFERENCES **REFERENCES** REFERENCES **REFERENCES** REFERENCES

Bloom, B.S., Ebgelhart, M., Furst, E., Hill, W. and Krathwohl, D. (1956) *Taxonomy of educational objectives: The classification of educational goals, Handbook 1: Cognitive Domain*. New York: Longmans Green.

Newmann, F. & Associates (1996) *Authentic achievement*. San Francisco, Jossey-Bass Publishers.

QCA (2008a) *A fresh approach to assessment*. www.qca.org.uk/qca_16883.aspx

QCA (2008b) *APP: Assessment at the heart of learning*. www.qca.org.uk/qca_16884.aspx

FURTHER READING FURTHER READING **FURTHER READING** FURTHER READING

Black, P. et al. (2003) *Assessment for learning: Putting it into practice*. Buckingham: Open University Press.

Brooks, V. (2002) *Assessment in secondary schools: The new teachers' guide to monitoring, assessment, recording, reporting and accountability*. Milton Keynes: Open University Press.

Clark, S. (2001) *Unlocking formative assessment*. London: Hodder Murray.

Clark, S. (2004) *Formative assessment in the secondary classroom*. London: Hodder Murray.

Useful websites

Assessment Reform Group www.assessment-reform-group.org/

National Assessment Agency www.naa.org.uk

International Review of Curriculum and Assessment Frameworks Internet Archive www.inca.org.uk/

Assessment for Learning www.standards.dfes.gov.uk/personalisedlearning/five/afl/

7
Managing student behaviour

By the end of this chapter you should:

- have considered the wider context for behaviour management on your placement and ways in which your own situation as a trainee teacher affects behaviour;
- understand how teachers use their own behaviour and responses to improve the behaviour of their students;
- know more about ways in which good behaviour for learning can be established and how problem behaviours can be reduced and de-escalated;
- have considered when and how to use the school's sanctions and disciplinary referral systems;
- be able to identify behaviour situations where specialist guidance is required.

This chapter addresses the following Professional Standards for QTS:

Q1, Q2, Q4, Q5 , Q10, Q21(b), Q30, Q31

Introduction

As a trainee teacher you will be concerned about establishing and maintaining good behaviour. Your teacher training course will almost certainly offer extended input to help you reflect on the possible causes of poor behaviour in school and on ways in which you can make a positive impact on the behaviour of the students in your care. The purpose of this chapter is to allow you to focus on ways in which you can bring what you have learnt into practice effectively, avoiding some of the stress factors associated with behaviour management in school.

Behaviour in context

Behaviour in the school environment

Schools differ greatly in terms of the situations they present for behaviour management. These differences relate to expectations within the students' lives at home, class sizes, age groups, tradition and ethos, and the basic nature of the school building (for example, whether students are required to move in large groups along narrow corridors, or whether extensive travel on a 'split-site campus' is involved). In some schools the behaviour policy is central to the day-to-day business of teaching and learning, and to the management of the student community, whereas in others a 'light touch' seems to be all that is required in this respect. For trainee teachers these differences present a real challenge.

Much of the skill of behaviour management relates to the development of a complex network of teacher strategies which must gradually become 'second nature' in their application. A good analogy would be learning to drive – a learner driver will develop a range of procedures and responses designed to deal with potentially problematical driving conditions and will begin to apply them automatically. For both the teacher and the driver there will be times where a decision is required as to what strategy or strategies will be used, but decision-making will rest on the platform of good practice which has been developed to meet more common circumstances.

The behaviour management strategies which you draw upon in the initial stages of your training may be relatively limited or misapplied. In a school situation requiring strong behaviour management, problems will continue to occur until you have broadened your repertoire and until you are applying strategies appropriately. In a school where just a light touch is needed, it takes a very conscious effort to develop the strategies which would help you to manage behaviour elsewhere – but you must make this effort if you are to meet the standards for QTS.

PRACTICAL TASK PRACTICAL TASK PRACTICAL TASK PRACTICAL TASK PRACTICAL TASK

At the beginning of each of your teaching placements you should:

- find out about typical domestic and community situations for groups of students in the school and consider what implications this information has for behaviour management;
- broaden your consideration to include any school-related issues which affect student behaviour;
- read the school's behaviour management policy and identify: (a) what values are reflected in the policy, (b) what expectations for teachers are established by the policy, and (c) what support for teachers is outlined within the policy.

Learning to teach and the effects on student behaviour

When your school mentors identify the class groups for your training timetable, they will be concerned to ensure that any disruption to teaching and learning is minimal. Working with a trainee teacher can be a boost for a group as students respond well to fresh ideas which stimulate learning, but there is a risk that any lack of awareness of the students' needs, or any unsatisfactory aspects of your teaching, will detract from learning and destabilise behaviour. When reflecting on any poor behaviour in your classes, you need to decide whether you are the key factor rather than the students.

Whilst you are in the familiarisation stage of working with particular students, you must look closely at their identified needs. The class teacher, form tutor, members of the support team and the school's special educational needs co-ordinator (SENCo) must be consulted in this respect. You will need to find out about students in your classes who have:

- medical conditions;
- psychological needs;
- welfare needs;
- relationship problems;
- habitual behavioural responses;
- specific learning difficulties (possibly managed through an Individual Education Plan);
- very high ability or talent in your subject.

Your management of the class, and the learning activities which you plan for them, must take this range of needs into account or poor behavioural responses will increase. You should also ensure that you are picking up information on students' needs from staff briefing sessions, from email and electronic bulletins and through the staff mail system. (You will need to make an arrangement with your class teacher partners for new information and information updates to be passed on to you.)

You must also ensure that your teaching really does promote learning, and that weaker aspects are dealt with speedily through a cycle of evaluation, professional development and re-establishment. If ineffective teaching continues, behaviour is likely to deteriorate.

Finally, you must remember that teaching is an interpersonal activity, and your students will be greatly affected by the relationships which you foster through your teaching style.

CASE STUDY

The following commentary comes from a trainee teacher's assessment profile provided by her subject mentor in school.

Elaine has developed a very good rapport with students of all ages. Her delivery has vitality and humour. She communicates information and task instructions clearly, and frequently plans to engage interest at the beginning of a lesson with a fascinating piece of information or a high interest scenario. Wherever possible she includes links to the students' interests in the ongoing development of her lesson.

Elaine involves students in helpful workplace routines, which are well practised and conducted efficiently.

She regularly checks for understanding and is flexible in her response, bearing in mind the perceived needs of students needing further assistance or explanation. The strengths and achievements of her students are appropriately recognised and weaknesses are dealt with in a constructive manner. Her outlook is always positive.

Elaine does teach some class groups where behaviour can potentially be challenging, but her students usually exhibit constructive learning behaviour in response to her well-developed interpersonal skills.

At this stage you may wish to consider whether you share some of Elaine's strengths and attributes. Decide what steps could be taken to improve your interpersonal skills where needs have been identified.

Moving on
In the later stages of your training, re-audit your interpersonal skills and decide what areas you would still wish to develop.

Proactive behaviour management

The 4 Rs – rights, responsibilities, rules and routines

Teachers who are skilful behaviour managers will spend a significant amount of time at the beginning of the school year focusing on the rights of people in the classroom and consequent responsibilities, rules and routines with their groups (Rogers, 2007). In schools which are involved in an assertive discipline programme (Canter and Canter, 2001) or which use elements of this programme, there will be a focus on negotiating an appropriate set of rules with each class. Responsibilities and routines will be clearly established with the group, and here too there is likely to be discussion and negotiation with the students entering into an agreement on specific protocols.

When you are familiarising yourself with a class which you will later teach, it is essential that you pick up on work which has been done on the establishment of responsibilities, rules and routines, and how this has been achieved, so that you can reinforce and develop these crucial elements of proactive behaviour management in your own work. Details should be added to the class notes which you keep in your teaching files.

Establishing the 4Rs will have very little effect in itself, however. The agreement stands at the beginning of a teaching process designed to establish appropriate behaviour or to improve the behaviour of individuals and of groups. Teaching good behaviour is very like teaching your subject. In your lessons you will refer back to your learning objectives and encourage students to assess their achievements in this respect. To teach good behaviour, you will need to ensure that the responsibilities, rules and routines established for the class remain apparent as you move forward, referring to what has been agreed at appropriate points and offering commentary and positive feedback. You will also need to reward good behaviour: you should look at the range of rewards recommended by the school you are working with and ensure that your use of rewards covers sustained good behaviour and improved behaviour in a similar way to the recognition of good and improved working outcomes.

If your focus on the 4Rs is successful, the students' behaviour will improve in targeted areas, and it will be important to go back and review class needs to establish new directions for behavioural improvement. This is quite a difficult task for a trainee teacher, and it is perhaps something which you should do in collaboration with the class teacher concerned. You should, however, be able to use the students' growing acceptance of the connection between rule-governed behaviour and effective learning experiences to negotiate specific sets of rules to cover specialised activities in your lessons – e.g. to cover group discussion or presentation work where there is a need for students to listen carefully, contribute as appropriate and show respect for the work and views of others; to cover practical sessions where safety is a prime concern; or to cover activities which involve movement around the school. Rules which are negotiated on an *ad hoc* basis, immediately before the experience concerned, can readily be drawn upon to condition learning behaviour.

Overall it's important to remember not to let earlier work on the 4 Rs 'go cold' – to be effective the proactive teaching of behaviour needs to be constantly reinforced and developed, and gains need to be recognised and rewarded.

Other proactive behaviour management techniques

In addition to work on the 4 Rs, there is a wide range of proactive behaviour management techniques which teachers can use. The following ideas are particularly helpful.

- Adopt well thought-out procedures for the arrival of your students at the lesson, and for their dismissal, as it is here that the teacher can create a real sense of order, develop one-to-one contact with students, and reinforce rules and routines.
- Plan for effective management of resources.
- Scan the classroom at very regular intervals and give positive recognition to students on task. This will convince others that there is no scope for misbehaviour as you are fully aware of what is happening around the room.

- Adopt a 'good outcome' stance: use 'thank you' rather than 'please' when making requests or giving instructions, thereby assuming compliance, and put assured focus on what it will be like when the students are self-managing positively rather than introducing possibilities for misbehaviour into what you have to say.
- Use praise and recognition regularly to reinforce compliant behaviour, but remember that the praise given should not be disproportionate to the achievement concerned. You can offer a 'recognition plus target' statement for more limited behavioural achievements (e.g. *You've settled down to work well now, John. See if you can develop those ideas further.*)

PRACTICAL TASK PRACTICAL TASK **PRACTICAL TASK** PRACTICAL TASK **PRACTICAL TASK**

Use the sheet below to help you to focus on an extended range of proactive behaviour management techniques when observing colleagues who are skilful in this respect.

Focus for proactive behaviour management	Seen ✓	How did the teacher promote good learning behaviour?
Arrival of students at lesson/entry to classroom		
Reference to established rights and responsibilities, rules and routines		
Use of noise-level guide chart		
Involvement of group in rule creation and usage		
Seating arrangements		
Taking register		
Distribution of materials		
Gaining attention of class		
Voice and tone		
Scanning to check behaviour and positive comment		
Use of countdown or other prearranged signal to obtain silence		
Time management		
Management of transition between activities		
Teacher's movement around classroom/workspace		
Use of student names		
Use of eye contact and pause		
'Good outcome' stance		
Appropriate behaviour discussed and acknowledged		
Use of reward/praise/recognition for good work and effort of individuals		
Use of reward/praise/recognition for good behaviour of individuals		
Retrieval of materials		
Dismissal from lesson		

Moving on

In the later stages of your training, ask a fellow trainee or a teacher to observe your lesson using this sheet, and review your developing skills in this area.

- Which proactive behaviour management strategies are well used in your own teaching? Which strategies do you need to introduce or improve?
- Establish SMART (specific, measurable, realistic and time-framed) targets for development.

Moving on
In the later stages of your training, review your development against these targets.

Responding to poor behaviour

Ongoing attention to students' needs, to the features of your own lesson planning and presentation, and to proactive behaviour management should improve behaviour in your classes, but there will clearly be times when you will need to respond to poor behaviour.

The level of response

There are a number of 'judgement calls' here. You need to decide when the response to poor behaviour should be to find a way of getting the student back on task, when the school's system of teacher-imposed sanctions or referrals should be used, and when the behaviour is so extreme that you need to enlist the help of more senior colleagues, or of specialised staff. There will also be occasions when the best response to poor behaviour at a low level will simply be to ignore it, because it is safe and morally appropriate to do so and because any intervention would disrupt class learning to a far greater extent than allowing the behaviour to continue.

Low-level interventions

In most lessons, by far the greater proportion of poor behaviour is likely to be at a low level and requires a matching low-level intervention on your part, rather than recourse to sanctions. Your priorities should be to get the student or students back on task and to put in hand any necessary follow-up in ways which do not add to the disruption in learning.

You will therefore need to ensure that you are developing a range of responses to behaviour at the lowest level of intervention. The following steps can usually be taken without adding to any existing disturbance.

- Learn the names of your students and use them when picking up on poor behaviour.
- Scan the room very regularly (every minute or two) to spot the development of off-task behaviour.
- If a student is off-task, identify the student by name and use sustained eye contact and frown, or use strategic pause if you are speaking, to register disapproval and prompt the resumption of work.
- Use the student's name followed by 'the police officer's hand' (bend arm upwards and flatten palm outwards like a police officer stopping traffic) as a widely recognised indication that noise or off-task behaviour must stop.
- Move your position in class to target 'hot spots', standing behind chatterers or to the side of students who are obviously not on task.
- Re-target the student's work, making an appropriate note of target and time on their work if possible.

Persistent behaviour which is still at a fairly low level will require a more sustained verbal response, or further action, which may add to the disruption in learning for the class as a whole, but here your reasoning must be that the added disruption will be temporary. If your intervention is successful you will improve the situation overall. Ensure that in responding to this type of behaviour you are brief and assertive. You should indicate why the behaviour is unacceptable, relating this to the 4Rs if possible. Give a positive instruction associated with learning goals, together with a time limit in which at least the first stages of renewed work should be completed. If you feel that further reinforcement is necessary, give a clear warning as to what you will do if the student does not comply with your instructions; this should involve a proportionate sanction such as loss of privileges, moving away from peers, the loss of social time in order to complete work, etc., rather than something more suitable for more severe misbehaviour. (Redirecting students in this way does not always have to be done from the front of the class or with a volume that makes what you are doing disruptive to everyone. When the students are working individually or in groups, you can deal with individuals by moving closer to them and speaking quietly, but in an authoritative tone.)

De-escalating the response to intervention

Sometimes teachers find themselves led into a situation with a student which escalates, and poor student behaviour which was initially at a lower level becomes very serious because both parties (student and teacher) have allowed things to get out of hand. Avoid this by ensuring that you do not enter into an argument with a student, or use approaches (e.g. humiliation or aggression) which will result in a 'fight or flight' reaction. Try to de-escalate situations which are moving up the levels of response by:

- demonstrating respect for the student when giving counter-instructions – avoiding sarcasm, posturing or rhetorical questions which will quickly damage relationships;
- using assertive statements which link your instruction to rules which are agreed or accepted within the school and within the group and which pick up the logic of the agreement; sometimes this message is delivered through the notion of the student's behavioural choices, e.g. *If you choose to go on disturbing others, remember that you will also be choosing to stay back at break*);
- using assertive language (e.g. make use of the word 'need' as it relates to a firm chain of response linked to apparently accepted points – *You need to work very quietly now so that you can complete this by breaktime without disturbing others*);
- using a question rather than an accusation – *How can you work in ways that won't disturb others so much?* (remember to avoid rhetorical questions);
- accepting an element of the student's complaint in your response to side-step further disagreement – e.g. *Maybe other folk have been making a noise, but I do need you to...*;
- reasserting an earlier point relating simply to the need to complete work and allow other students to do so, rather than by responding to escalation on the part of the student;
- using the 'broken record technique' – i.e. simply reasserting up to three times, in a somewhat more emphatic tone each time, what the student should be doing and why (if this is going to work, you should not need to repeat the statement more than three times);
- giving an instruction, pausing and using eye contact with the student, and then turning and walking away to visibly release the potential conflict.

School sanction and referral systems

Although most of the poor behaviour you will meet in class is at a relatively low level, some misbehaviour is totally unacceptable and it is here that you should draw on the help provided by the recognised sanction and disciplinary referral systems. Misbehaviour which falls into this category includes very persistent and deliberate nuisance behaviour which continues to disrupt the learning of other students despite your best endeavours in terms of low-level responses; abusive behaviour (to the teacher or to other students); gross or lewd behaviour; aggressive or threatening behaviour; and deliberate bullying. Schools offer clear guidance in terms of the use of sanctions and referral in situations of these types , and many now work with a consequences system which offers whole-school support for the teacher when it becomes necessary to use out-of-lesson sanctions. Make sure that you have a good working familiarity with the system used in your placement school.

Specialist support

Most young people are able to take responsibility for their own actions and exert self-control, although at times they need a reminder about how their behaviour affects others. There are exceptions to this, however, in that some students have medical or psychological conditions which influence their behaviour, or have developed pathological patterns of behaviour due to very difficult circumstances in their lives. Earlier in this chapter, it was recommended that you should seek information on the individual needs of students within your classes, and as you begin to teach you should draw upon the advice given in this respect and continue to seek help and guidance where necessary. Whilst you cannot allow students who have extreme needs, and who consequently adopt extreme behaviours, to disrupt the learning of others, your SENCo should be able to recommend practices which will make the learning situation more amenable for the students concerned, and will advise on what steps to take if you need to go beyond your own devices in the classroom. Continue to work closely with the group's timetabled class teacher, your head of department and the special educational needs team to develop supportive programmes for students with extreme needs – and don't hesitate to advise these colleagues if specific situations are too difficult for you to manage.

Frequently asked questions

I know that a great deal of the misbehaviour in my classes is because I'm a trainee teacher and new to the school. The students are 'trying it on' with me. In view of the levels of disturbance, would it be better for me to stick with a range of intervention levels, or should I show that I can be really strict and impose detentions and other school consequences to turn things around?

When students 'try it on' with trainee teachers, it is often to see if the trainee can cope well with the management of low-level disciplinary problems. If you move up the ladder of response too quickly, imposing detentions, seeking assistance from more senior members of staff, or using referred punishments within a 'consequences' system when these measures are unnecessary, you will lose the respect of many of your students because they will feel that you do not have the behaviour management skills required.

What is 'working noise', and how can I achieve it with a talkative class?

If you want students to discuss their learning together, you must establish appropriate expectations. Ideally, students should not engage in conversation beyond their immediate pairing or group, they must lower their voices so that anyone passing can hear the buzz of conversation but cannot catch the drift of what is being said, and they must remain on task within the framework of the discussion. Collaborative activities will provide you with a good opportunity to negotiate an appropriate set of working rules with your class – but you will need to work hard to establish the rules by recognising and praising conforming behaviour, and by using a good range of low-level interventions to cut back on minor disruptions.

> *One of my classes is particularly challenging. It's often difficult to know who is responsible for disruptions and most of the students become involved. School policy discourages full class detentions, but I am tempted to use this measure. Are there occasions where this is appropriate?*

You must never be tempted to arrange a detention for a whole class – this would be an admission that your scanning techniques had not enabled you to pinpoint who is to blame for disruption, and you would find it difficult to deal with the resulting hardening of student attitudes and complaints coming in from parents. Take advice from the class teacher with regard to teaching and learning strategies, and provision for individual students in this group. You will need to use the full range of behaviour management strategies, but as a priority ensure that you are working proactively in this respect in order to create space for high-quality teaching and learning.

A SUMMARY OF **KEY POINTS**

> Ensure that you are fully aware of the needs of specific students in your group.
> Check that the features of your lesson planning are appropriate, and that your demeanour works positively in the context of behaviour management.
> Teach behaviour through the negotiation and establishment of rights, responsibilities, rules and routines.
> Follow up with two further Rs – recognition and reward for good and improved behaviour.
> Use a range of proactive behaviour management strategies to prevent the occurrence of poor behaviour.
> Deal with low-level behaviour problems with low-level interventions, and work to prevent the escalation of a student's response to intervention.
> Ensure that your verbal interventions are assertive rather than aggressive or high-handed.
> Use the school's sanctions and disciplinary referral systems appropriately.

REFERENCES REFERENCES **REFERENCES** REFERENCES **REFERENCES** REFERENCES

Canter, L. and Canter, M. (2001) *Assertive discipline: Positive behaviour management for today's classroom*, (3rd edition). Santa Monica: Lee Canter.
Rogers, Bill (2007) *Behaviour Management: A whole-school approach* London:Paul Chapman/Sage.

FURTHER READING FURTHER READING **FURTHER READING** FURTHER READING

Cowley, S. (2001) *Getting the buggers to behave.* London: Continuum.
Hook, P. and Vass A. (2000a) *Confident classroom leadership*. London: David Fulton.
Hook, P. and Vass, A. (2006) *Creating winning classrooms*. London: David Fulton.
Hook, P. and Vass, A. (2002) *Teaching with influence*. London: David Fulton.

Useful websites

A compendium of information on student behaviour and behaviour management for trainee teachers and teacher educators – www.behaviour4learning.ac.uk
Information on special educational needs related to behaviour can also be found on the website for the Office for Advice, Assistance, Support and Information on Special Needs – www.oaasis.co.uk

8
Your pastoral role

By the end of this chapter you should:

- be aware of different models of pastoral organisation in school;
- understand the place and purposes of pastoral work;
- understand your role as a tutor and as a member of the pastoral team;
- know how to become an effective tutor;
- understand the links between pastoral organisation and PSHE/citizenship.

This chapter addresses the following Professional Standards for QTS:

Q1, Q2, Q3(a), Q4, Q5, Q21(a,b)

Introduction

The purpose of this chapter is to introduce you to, and give you an overall view of, your role as a form tutor and member of the pastoral team in school. Almost all teachers have a responsibility as a form tutor in addition to their subject-teaching role. It is an aspect of their work which many enjoy. During your school placements you are likely to be attached to a form group and to gradually begin to take on the responsibilities of the tutor.

The pastoral system: what is its purpose?

All secondary schools in England have some form of pastoral system. This is not the case with all school systems. In some countries, pastoral work does not form part of the teacher's role.

> **PRACTICAL TASK** PRACTICAL TASK PRACTICAL TASK PRACTICAL TASK PRACTICAL TASK
>
> Before going further, write down your own answer to the question: what is the purpose of a school's pastoral system?

It is likely that you have included something about the 'whole child' and focused on students' well-being and overall development. You may have included the word 'care' and emphasised personal relationships and the development of the young adult as a person, not just as a learner. You may also have included some idea of the pastoral system being instrumental in the development and maintenance of good behaviour in the school and the creation of the school ethos. All these are important features of pastoral care. However, in recent years there has been an increasing focus on the links between these 'caring' and 'discipline' aspects and the importance of the pastoral system in supporting academic achievement. This view sees the pastoral structure as essentially underpinning the academic structure, with one of its main purposes being to ensure that students are able to fulfil their academic potential through academic tutoring and monitoring of achievement. This shift in focus has been brought about by the government focus on raising standards, increased availability of assessment data, resulting in the use of predictive targets and grades and the benchmarking of schools and students against local and national performance.

Pastoral organisation: possible models

Schools have choices to make in the ways they structure the pastoral system. A key issue for schools in making this choice centres on the idea of continuity in the tutor–student–parent relationship. Schools will have a view on how important they think this continuity is in supporting students in their development as young adults and in enabling them to achieve their potential academically. However, some would argue that changes of tutor can be beneficial as students 'outgrow' the relationship they may have formed with an individual tutor during their early years and are ready to move on, or for students whose relationship with their tutor is not productive.

There are two main structures in use, each of which has implications for the way students feel they 'belong' in the school.

Vertical structure

In this structure, tutor groups include students from all the year groups in the school. The tutor remains with these students throughout their time in the school, each year losing students from the top of the age range and gaining students who are joining the school in Year 7. In larger schools, a vertical structure may also involve a 'house' system with students and tutors belonging to a house. Siblings from one family may belong to the same tutor group or at least the same house. Thus, tutors can build strong relationships with parents and students over time. Older students can act as confidante, friend, role model, mentor and, on occasion, 'protector' for younger students. This can help develop a sense of responsibility among older students towards 'their' younger students and can help the school to create a sense of cohesion. Extracurricular competitive activities between groups or houses are facilitated through this structure. From the tutor's viewpoint, they can see the development of 'their' tutees throughout the students' school career and are able to use this depth of knowledge to advantage. At any one point in the school year, when important decisions are to be made – for example, subject option choices in Year 9 – the tutor has only five or six students to focus on and so can give time to these as individuals. Students can develop a real sense of the way their career will progress as they see older students going through the various stages and decisions that occur through the school years.

Horizontal structure

In this structure, also called a year group structure, tutor groups contain students from one year only. Often, tutors remain with the same group for several years on a 'rolling' system. So, a tutor may remain with the group throughout Key Stage 3 or perhaps throughout Key Stages 3 and 4 before again taking on a Year 7 group. The tutor belongs to a year group team of tutors led by a head of year or head of Key Stage. The advantage of this system is that all the students in the group are likely to have similar issues to have to deal with, whether administrative or personal, making it easier for the tutor to focus on and support students. Year group assemblies can also have a clear focus designed to address the particular needs of the age group. Tutors may become knowledgeable and skilled in dealing with specific areas such as transition from the primary to secondary phase, selecting options or making post-16 choices. Post-16 groups are often taken by a dedicated team of tutors who have in-depth knowledge of the higher education system and training and workplace options. The year group system has been the most popular during the past two decades, but some schools are again showing an interest in mixed age groupings.

Your role as a tutor

You chose to become a teacher of your subject. Your degree studies will have prepared you with the subject knowledge you need to be able to teach this. Becoming a form tutor is not something which is the subject of any degree but it is a role for which you need to develop a body of knowledge and skills.

In the primary phase, the student spends all or most of the week with one person: their class teacher. The development of a close and supportive relationship is facilitated by this frequent contact. There are plenty of opportunities for the teacher to observe the student and gain knowledge of the student's learning achievements, preferences, social relationships and family circumstances. In the secondary phase, as form tutor, you are the one staff member who sees the student each day, usually the first staff contact the student has each morning. You may not teach the student but you are expected to have detailed knowledge of them as a learner and as an individual. Your contact is relatively limited but you do need to be able to develop a close and supportive relationship with each member of your tutor group. The tutor is key to enabling the student to become a full and integrated member of the school community and to supporting them in achieving their potential.

Key tasks of a form tutor

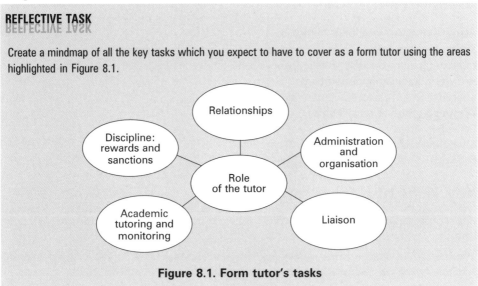

Figure 8.1. Form tutor's tasks

Now check your responses against the following list. This is not exclusive and you may have items on your list which do not appear here.

Relationships

Building relationships:
- with students/parents
- between students
- within the tutor group

Monitoring/advising on relationships between students
Monitoring social integration
Advising on personal/family issues
Establishing a sense of belonging to the school community and ownership of the tutor room.

Discipline: rewards and sanctions

Enforcing school rules; e.g. uniform
Collating school rewards/sanctions
Giving praise/reprimands
Monitoring detentions.

Academic tutoring and monitoring

Monitoring achievement and setting targets
Collation of data/RAISEONLINE
Monitoring subject reports and writing tutor reports
Homework monitoring
Diary/planner check.

Liaison

Parents
Head of year/house/Key Stage
SENCo/LSA
Subject teachers
Learning mentors.

Administration and organisation

Taking register
Monitoring attendance/collecting absence letters
Arranging tutor-group assemblies
Checking uniform and equipment/planners/diaries
Informing group of bulletins/daily reports
Collecting money
Giving out newsletters
Maintaining tutor group notice board.

Key skills of a form tutor

REFLECTIVE TASK

Consider the list of tasks above and any you have added. Make a list of the key skills and personal attributes which you think you will need as a form tutor.

Administration and organisation

This is likely to loom large in the proportion of time taken up from that officially allocated to tutor work. Taking the register and collecting, filing and chasing absence notes are likely to be among the first tutor actions that you undertake whilst training as these do not involve your getting to know the tutor group or having developed relationships with individuals. Nevertheless, they are important procedures. Recording and monitoring attendance is a legal responsibility. Your placement schools will have procedures set in place for this and you need to ensure that you understand and follow them.

Similarly, weekly checking of homework diaries, checking uniform – particularly its correct wearing – and collecting in of reward or sanction points, distribution of notices and collection of reply slips are likely to be among your early tutor responsibilities on placement. Do not dismiss these as trivial: good organisation and administration are vital to the smooth running of a school and upholding its ethos, and having systems set in place will allow you to spend more time on those aspects of the tutor's role which you may find more rewarding and interesting.

If you are to have time for the caring and nurturing side of your form tutor role, you will need to have well-developed organisational skills in order to deal effectively and quickly with the many administrative tasks facing you. A good filing system for absence and other notes, a methodical approach to noting who has returned which reply slip from home, for collating merits and sanctions and recording progress against targets will save time and enable you to give accurate data to your colleagues. You will also need a secure, confidential method for recording any concerns noted by you or expressed to you by colleagues.

PRACTICAL TASK PRACTICAL TASK **PRACTICAL TASK** PRACTICAL TASK **PRACTICAL TASK**

Early in each placement, find out your school's systems for recording and monitoring attendance. Look at the patterns of attendance for individuals in the group to which you are assigned.

Talk to the group's tutor about the administrative demands made of tutors in the school and gain advice about how to organise these tasks and records.

Moving on

In the later stages of your training, devise systems to keep records and try these out for their practical impact and information value.

Interpersonal skills

You will need good interpersonal skills in order to build effective relationships with students, with parents and with staff. You will need to support, guide and motivate students. Some will need your encouragement in order to develop stamina as learners; others will need firm guidance in developing appropriate responses to school and class rules and appropriate behaviour for learning. In such cases you will need to be able to uphold the school rules firmly whilst avoiding damaging your relationship with the student. You will aim to teach your tutees respect: of themselves, their fellow students, staff, property, society and their families.

You may need to act as a buffer and intermediary between a student and other members of staff, sometimes acting as advocate for the student, sometimes reinforcing the position of the member of staff. Remember that even when you may privately agree that the student has a genuine concern, you will need to be professional regarding what you say to the student about that staff member.

You will also need to develop relationships with parents, helping them to have realistic expectations of achievement and to understand the education system. You will often be the first point of contact for concerned parents worried about their child's performance or behaviour or the impact of family issues upon the student. It may be you who initiates contact, although whilst in training you should ensure that you take advice and adopt the school policy regarding such contact. You will need to deal with issues sensitively.

Listening

Are you a good listener? And approachable? These are key skills for a form tutor. Students frequently choose their form tutor as the person with whom they wish to discuss problems or important decisions. This may involve issues of friendship, difficulties with subjects or staff or at home, bullying or personal problems, decisions regarding option choices or career paths. Your advice may be sought or it may simply be the act of listening which is required. Students will want to be assured that you will be fair, consistent, positive and will not bear grudges or be judgemental. Above all, students will want to feel that their tutor is trustworthy to keep their confidences except where these have to be shared elsewhere, to give sound advice and to carry out agreed actions. Remember that you should never promise that you will not disclose the confidence to anyone else as you may need to inform the member of staff responsible for child protection. You should be clear about this to students who ask you to promise not to tell anyone before they disclose a concern.

PRACTICAL TASK PRACTICAL TASK PRACTICAL TASK PRACTICAL TASK PRACTICAL TASK

Early in each placement:

- talk to the nominated teacher responsible for child protection so that you understand procedures regarding pupils disclosing information;
- talk to your mentor so that you understand procedures regarding the school policy on contacting parents.

Keeping an overview and keeping a distance

You will need to keep an overview of each tutee's progress and attitude to learning, together with an understanding of anything which impacts upon this. You will need to keep your eyes and ears open as you go around the school, being aware of how your tutees are faring both academically and socially, noticing when they have a difficulty of some sort and taking action where appropriate. You should aim to be proactive rather than simply reactive (although this too will be necessary at times).

Your relationship with your tutor group is likely to be more informal and closer than your relationship with a teaching group. You will need, however, to keep a professional distance: being friendly and approachable without being a friend. You may have to tackle a student who contravenes the school dress code, through wearing of jewellery, for example, enforcing the school rules firmly, yet also be open to listening to them sensitively and giving advice. Your role is not that of social worker or peer or friend. You are a teacher and as such must ensure that there is the professional distance expected of the teacher/student relationship and that you know when to refer an issue to another professional. The tutor has a role to play in delivering the outcomes of the *Every Child Matters* agenda.

CASE STUDY

Ryan is in Year 10. His form tutor is worried because he is repeatedly late for school. Ryan's tutor knows his home life is difficult and believes he may be helping to care for his younger sister. The tutor has spoken to him before, but the situation has not improved and so the tutor asks to see Ryan at lunchtime.

The tutor is careful not to be accusatory or to begin the conversation by reprimanding Ryan for lateness and begins by asking how things are for Ryan now in school, then steering the conversation towards how things are at home. Ryan confesses he is struggling to get to school on time because he has to get his Year 5 sister to school. His mother is working early shifts as a cleaner and her latest boyfriend left a few weeks ago. Ryan says his mother is usually too tired in the evening to do much so he ends up doing a lot of the housework, which interferes with his homework. School work isn't a high priority.

The tutor knows that the aim must be to get Ryan to school on time – punctuality is an important attribute and when in work Ryan will need to be on time – and able to achieve his potential. The tutor could make contact with Ryan's mother but decides as a first step to try to help Ryan cope with his family responsibilities and with being punctual and achieving at school. The tutor gives practical suggestions such as ensuring that Ryan's sister gets her school things ready the night before to make mornings less pressured, looking to see whether Ryan can drop his sister off at a friend's house rather than take her all the way to school and, if this is not possible, offers help in negotiating with the primary school for Ryan to drop his sister off early. The tutor also arranges a quiet space for Ryan to do his homework in the lunch and break times and mediates with staff so that Ryan has extra time for homework or a lighter homework demand where possible. The tutor continues to monitor the situation and to offer Ryan support and encouragement to achieve his potential and meet his family responsibilities. The tutor also makes a note to talk to Ryan's mother at the next parents' evening.

Links with raising achievement

Target-setting

There is an increasing emphasis on raising and supporting achievement and the key function of schools being to enable pupils to fulfil their potential. The central purpose of the pastoral system, and the tutor in particular, is seen as removing or mediating barriers to achievement. Many schools now hold interviews at several points in the year where tutors meet with parents and pupils in order to review progress and set targets in subject areas. The tutor is the key person who holds an overview of the pupil's achievements, attitude and personal background and can feedback on progress and discuss what can be done to improve. This develops the tutor's role, strengthening the tutor's relationship with the pupil and their parents and making firm links between pastoral care and academic achievement. In order to carry out these interviews effectively, the tutor needs to be provided with data and be able to interpret this for pupils and parents. Accurate record-keeping and close monitoring of progress are vital.

Early in training: Talk with the tutor to whose group you are attached about the way in which data is gathered and used by form tutors, and the way the interview is prepared for and conducted.

Later in training: Shadow a tutor during the preparation and conduct of a target setting interview.

Learning mentors

Learning mentors were introduced as part of the Excellence in Cities (EiC) programme. They provide a bridge across the academic and pastoral and aim to offer support and guidance and remove barriers to learning. Students selected for this initiative are those who need to raise their aspirations or who are showing signs of disaffection and lack of motivation which act as barriers to their achieving their full potential. As form tutor, you will want to monitor the progress of students engaged in this mentoring, being aware of when the meetings are taking place and encouraging students to attend.

Consider your response as a tutor to the situation which follows.

- What preparation will you do before speaking to Martin?
- What information will you need to hand and where will you find it?
- How will you broach the topic with Martin?
- What follow-up action will you take?
- Would engaging with a learning mentor be of benefit to Martin?

Martin is a Year 12 student in your tutor group. You have recently been made aware that he is working 20 hours a week on shifts in a local supermarket. Subject teachers have approached you with concerns that he is underachieving on his AS (advanced subsidiary) courses. Martin has missed several coursework deadlines and has told teachers that he can easily catch up but work has still not been forthcoming. Martin has not met his targets for the past term. You have looked at the data concerning his current achievement and his projected targets for the AS exams. You ask to see him. He is not aware of the reason you want to talk to him.

Links with PSHE

Schools vary in the way they deliver PSHE (see Chapter 9). In many schools, PSHE is delivered by form tutors during an extended form tutor time or dedicated PSHE time. Tutors, who know the 'whole child', may well be able to provide a safe and supportive environment for discussion of what can be sensitive issues. Where PSHE is delivered through an extended tutor time, there is a temptation to use this time to catch up with administrative tasks. You will need to consider how you will ensure that you allow time for PSHE and how you will use your knowledge of your tutees to create an open and safe environment for discussion. You will also need to consider what subject and pedagogical knowledge and skills you will need to acquire in order to deliver PSHE effectively.

Frequently asked questions

I get on well with the form I am attached to in tutor time, but when I teach them behaviour is often poor and pupils are often off-task.

Revisit the section above on maintaining a professional distance, and Chapter 7 on behaviour management. Reflect upon the difference between 'being friendly' and 'being a friend' and put in place measures, both in tutor time and in teaching time to redefine and re-establish expectations.

> *I am attached to a tutor group which is known as difficult and I am always receiving complaints about them from other staff. What can I do to change this?*

Establishing a group ethos, setting high expectations, using rewards and sanctions is as important in tutor group as in class. In tutor time, incorporate some activities which will reinforce these.

> *I want to take 'my' tutor group on an outing to reinforce the group ethos. Can I take them ice-skating?*

You should consult the school policy here and take advice from your pastoral head. Whilst outings can be of enormous value to pupils and hugely enjoyable, they also carry weighty responsibilities and a risk assessment will have to be carried out.

A SUMMARY OF **KEY POINTS**

> Make sure you understand the key tasks and key skills of a form tutor. Consider how to develop your interpersonal and listening skills.

> Consider the boundaries of a form tutor's role and know when to pass on issues to other professionals.

> Give thought to the tutor room environment and how you enable students to feel ownership of the room.

> Speak to your mentor about the way in which the pastoral system in your placements supports achievement

> Gather information about whether your school links the pastoral system with the delivery of PSHE.

REFERENCES REFERENCES **REFERENCES** REFERENCES **REFERENCES** REFERENCES

DfES (2003) *Every Child Matters* www.everychild matters.gov.uk/publications

FURTHER READING FURTHER READING **FURTHER READING** FURTHER READING

Collins, U.M. and McNiff, J. (eds) (2002) *Re-thinking pastoral care*. London: Routledge.
Marland, M. and Rogers, R. (2004) *How to be a successful form tutor.* London: Continuum
Watson-Davies, R. (2005) *Form tutor's pocket book.* Alresford: Teachers' Pocketbooks.

Useful websites

www.napce.org.uk
    website of the National Association for Pastoral Care in Education
www.teacherstv/video/2749
Other video clips also available at the Teachers TV site
www.raiseonline.org/login.aspx?ReturnUrl=%2findex.aspx
    RAISEONLINE (Reporting and Analysis for Improvement through School Self-Evaluation) provides interactive analysis of school and pupil performance data.

9
SMSC, PSHE and citizenship

By the time you complete this chapter you should:

- understand your professional and statutory responsibilities in relation to SMSC, PSHE and citizenship;
- have identified how, where and when you can support the development of SMSC in your pupils;
- know the areas included in the PSHE and citizenship curriculums;
- understand the ways in which PSHE and citizenship are delivered in schools;
- have considered your own subject knowledge in relation to PSHE and citizenship;
- know how to document students' progress in relation to these to provide evidence for your training.

This chapter addresses the following Professional Standards for QTS:

Q3(a), Q7(a), Q15, Q18

Introduction

The three areas of SMSC (spiritual, moral, social and cultural education), PSHE (personal, social and health education) and citizenship can be the aspects of training to teach that are least focused on by both schools and trainees alike, possibly because you are so focused on learning to teach your subject well (unless you are training to be a citizenship teacher, of course). However, effective teachers take these elements of their role seriously, and are aware of when and how they can meaningfully integrate them into the pupils' learning experience.

What these three elements of educational provision recognise, and therefore remind us as teachers of, is that the education of young people is not purely about academic knowledge and skills. It is also about enabling young people to become independent adults who are able to take responsibility for themselves and be responsible to others in a wide range of situations; about developing as an individual; about growing into the person they are and will become. These elements of the teacher's job are just as important as, if not more important than, stuffing the pupils as full of curriculum content as possible.

This is of course not always easy to achieve in schools, especially when the league tables consistently emphasise academic performance and schools are judged on this. But Ofsted also inspects schools for the quality of their provision for PSHE, SMSC and Citizenship, and it is often the case that the majority of teaching staff will be involved in one or more of these elements of the school experience for pupils. So this is a part of your training that you cannot afford to ignore.

Approaches to SMSC, PSHE and citizenship during training

The first thing to identify when you have spent time organising your teaching timetable and pastoral attachment for the placement is: how does the school deliver each of these elements of the broader curriculum? (See Chapter 10 for more on this.) Different schools will employ different models for different reasons: many will deliver PSHE via the form tutor through an extended tutor period, while other schools will have one dedicated lesson per week or fortnight taught by a team of 'semi-specialists' or form tutors; SMSC may be delivered purely through the curriculum and assemblies, so may not be easily discernible to you; and citizenship may have a trained, dedicated teacher, or draw upon subject teachers to deliver the curriculum, or tutors to deliver citizenship within PSHE sessions.

You may need to be proactive when it comes to gaining experience of these three curriculum areas during placement. Although your subject mentor in school will organise a timetable for your subject teaching and pastoral experience, they may not provide for SMSC/PSHE/citizenship. Your professional mentor may incorporate them into your professional training programme in school. While it might be unrealistic to expect to gain experience of all three of these areas, depending on the length of a particular placement, it might be worthwhile trying to organise a period on your timetable that covers one area. During the early stage of your training this may be just to observe, while later you may wish to offer to teach, or support, a series of lessons.

REFLECTIVE TASK

Consider each area (PSHE/SMSC/Citizenship) in turn in relation to the following questions.

- What is your attitude to teaching this area? To its role in school life?
- What can you take from your knowledge of your subject pedagogy into delivering this area?
- When might you need to consider different pedagogic approaches than those you are used to in your subject? For example, drama, art, physical, media, ICT, discussion forums, and so on? How do you feel about this?
- Where can you get support for this if you are not feeling confident, or are unclear about using such approaches?
- How will you plan for classroom management when delivering this area?

It is important that you regard including one of these areas on your timetable as an opportunity, not a burden. It will bring breadth and scope to your teaching experience, your relationship with the pupils, and to your contribution to the school.

Spiritual, moral, social and cultural education

Schools have a legal duty to promote SMSC development in their pupils, and Ofsted will be looking for this during their inspections. To support schools in doing so, Ofsted has produced a document called *Promoting and Evaluating Pupils' Spiritual, Moral, Social and Cultural Development* which you may find useful to refer to.

There are two ways in which SMSC is commonly delivered: through the pastoral system, and through the subject curriculum. How schools do this is up to them, and you will need to investigate how each of your placement schools chooses to implement SMSC development. However, SMSC can be the most difficult of the three areas to really understand; again the Ofsted document above provides some definitions of the terms 'spiritual', 'moral', 'social' and 'cultural'; but you need to have a sense for yourself of what these mean in terms of the context of each school in which you are placed, as it will differ in each case.

REFLECTIVE TASK

What characteristics would you expect pupils to demonstrate who are developing:

- spiritually;
- morally;
- socially;
- culturally.

What are you aware that schools do to develop these? What do you think schools should be doing?

Delivering SMSC during placement

Once you are familiar with how your placement school delivers SMSC, you need to work with your mentors to understand how it impacts on your roles. You should be engaging with pupils both in curriculum and pastoral areas, and it is likely that SMSC will be accounted for in both of those, although in different ways. You need to be familiar with what is expected of you, and in later stages of your training to be proactive in identifying opportunities for incorporating SMSC development into your contact with pupils. But SMSC goes further than planned opportunities; it is inherent in the fabric of the school, in the school ethos, buildings, rules and traditions. When you join the school, even during placement, you add to that fabric, and you must both uphold and support the ethos of the school.

PRACTICAL TASK PRACTICAL TASK PRACTICAL TASK PRACTICAL TASK PRACTICAL TASK

- Make sure your professional mentor discusses SMSC during your professional training programme – if it is not on the programme, ask about it.
- Identify where your personal responsibilities will lie during this placement; in the pastoral system, the curriculum, in extracurricular activities?
- Identify who you need to talk to about your responsibilities for SMSC: the form tutor you are working with, your subject mentor, the pastoral team leader.
- Be prepared to plan – this is just as important with elements such as SMSC as it is for your subject, or your tutor group.

Moving on

SMSC is generally incorporated into the pastoral and curricular aspects of school, and so, as a teacher, you need to be both aware of when opportunities present in order to do so effectively, and how to balance the teaching of your subject or the demands of pastoral work with highlighting issues of SMSC development as they arise. You will need to discuss this with your subject mentor in relation to the material you will be teaching with each group, and anticipate possible areas for SMSC development, as they can be difficult to deal with 'on the spot' – but this is often where the most valuable learning opportunities occur for pupils, because they are in the context of the lesson.

Personal, social and health education (PSHE)

PSHE gives students the knowledge, understanding, attitudes and skills to live safely, productively and responsibly as adults. There are strong links between PSHE and the five key outcomes of *Every Child Matters*:

- be healthy;
- stay safe;
- enjoy and achieve;
- make a positive contribution;
- achieve economic well-being.

The relationship between PSHE and the school ethos is an important one. PSHE contributes to personal development and helps young people to explore and build their personal identity and confidence; to manage emotions and develop an understanding of themselves and others in order to develop relationships. In school this is achieved both through specific PSHE timetabled lessons, through learning opportunities across the curriculum and through special projects.

In many schools PSHE is delivered by form tutors. Often, the teacher in charge of PSHE provision decides the curriculum and provides resources to tutors. This can lead to a 'work-sheet' dependency approach and to boredom and lack of regard for the status of PSHE amongst students. To be successful and to ensure that pupils gain from PSHE lessons, you will need to give as much thought to planning and to preparation for these lessons as to those you teach in your specialist subject. In some schools PSHE is delivered by a small team of semi-specialists. If this is the case in your placement, you will need to ensure that you are involved in this team in order to gain experience of teaching PSHE.

There is no statutory curriculum for PSHE. However, there is non-statutory guidance, which complements the programmes for citizenship, and most schools use this to frame their provision The curriculum for PSHE, as part of the revised secondary curriculum (in schools from September 2008), has two programmes of study:

- personal well-being;
- economic well-being and financial capability.

As for all other subjects, the focus is on key concepts and processes. You should consider carefully the pedagogical approaches which are most effective in this area as they may not be those you commonly use in your subject teaching. Do you have the skills to promote discussion? Do you practise active listening and can you teach these skills to pupils?

PSHE usually includes the topic areas:

- sex and relationships education;
- drugs, alcohol and tobacco education;
- finance education;
- nutrition and physical activity;
- emotional health and well-being;
- safety.

The non-statutory guidance focuses on:

- giving students knowledge, skills and understanding;
- developing understanding of what constitutes a healthy and safe lifestyle and their choices in relation to this;
- developing effective relationships and respecting the differences between people;
- developing students' confidence and enabling them to make the most of their abilities.

Schools are also obliged to deliver careers education and citizenship and in many schools, these are also addressed within the general area of PSHE.

REFLECTIVE TASK

Audit your subject knowledge in each of these areas. Where will you need to gain knowledge?

Now consider your own feelings about each of these topics. How will you ensure that you do not impart your own prejudices and beliefs but enable students to form their own judgements?

What kind of pedagogical approaches will be most effective?

Developing your subject knowledge

Many beginning teachers feel that they need to acquire subject knowledge in order to teach PSHE topics effectively. Some aspects of sex education and drugs, alcohol and tobacco education are dealt with in the science curriculum, but other aspects are focused on within PSHE.

Sex and relationships education

Schools develop their own curriculum taking account of government guidelines. All schools must, however, deliver sex and relationships education. This curriculum should be inclusive of all students and should be culturally appropriate. Thus there will be differences between schools. You will need to be aware of the ethos and cultural background of the school in which you are working. Some factual aspects of sex education are dealt with within the statutory science curriculum. PSHE generally deals with physical and emotional development, sex, sexuality and sexual health. Be aware that parents can withdraw their children from the non-statutory elements of sex education.

Drugs, alcohol and tobacco education

Again, some aspects fall within the science curriculum. PSHE deals with the effects of substance use and abuse on both the individual and on society as part of enabling students to lead confident, safe, healthy and productive lives.

Finance education

Students are given the knowledge and understanding to develop financial capability and lead independent lives. There are close links with citizenship here.

Nutrition and physical activity

Some aspects of physical activity will be delivered through the physical education subject curriculum, but understanding what it means to be healthy and gaining the knowledge to make lifestyle choices in relation to nutrition and activity which lead to a healthy life fall within PSHE.

Emotional health and well-being

Students should be made aware of emotional health issues faced by all people, and given the capability to understand their own emotions and to support others.

Safety education

This is essentially about 'risk'. Students should be taught to recognise, assess and take action in regard to risk in their lives, at work, in sport and in leisure time.

PRACTICAL TASK PRACTICAL TASK PRACTICAL TASK PRACTICAL TASK PRACTICAL TASK

Access and read the PSHE curriculum.

Find out how your school delivers the PSHE curriculum and ensure that you are able to become involved through observation and group support.

Using your audit from the reflective task above, access one of the websites given at the end of this chapter and take action to develop your subject knowledge for areas where you are not confident.

Moving on

In the later stages of your training, arrange to plan, develop resources for and teach a series of PSHE lessons, ensuring that you take subject knowledge, pedagogical approach and your own attitudes and beliefs into account.

Assessing PSHE

This is a thorny issue for many schools and teachers. There is no set mode of assessment for PSHE. Schools are free to develop their own assessment framework. However, PSHE is normally reported upon to parents, and Ofsted will look at the effectiveness of the school's provision. You will need, therefore, to consider the issues of assessment, reporting and recording very carefully. There is guidance from the Qualifications and Curriculum Authority (QCA) on this, which emphasises the importance of assessment in planning, ensuring progression, acknowledging achievement and motivating students. The nature of the subject lends itself very well to AfL approaches (see Chapter 6).

PRACTICAL TASK PRACTICAL TASK PRACTICAL TASK PRACTICAL TASK PRACTICAL TASK

Find out how your school assesses, records and reports PSHE.

CASE STUDY

Ali, who has strong religious faith, has been asked to deliver sex and relationships education to a Year 9 group. This will include teaching about sexual relationships outside marriage, contraception and abortion. Ali feels uncertain about how to handle these issues, some aspects of which will conflict with Ali's own personal convictions. Ali consults the teacher in charge of the PSHE programme, who is willing to allow Ali to opt out of these lessons. However, she explains that it is not the role of teachers to give their own views or to promote one way of thinking as the 'right way', but to present the facts and to help students to understand that people hold very different views depending upon their own convictions, religious or otherwise. The teacher's role is to facilitate discussion so that students arrive at their own conclusions having considered the topic from different viewpoints and also are able to respect the views of others.

After giving the matter some thought, Ali decides to teach the lessons and prepares carefully to ensure that students receive factual evidence and, through research and structured debate, are encouraged to develop their own opinions and respect those of others. In this way, at no time is there a requirement to promote views which are in conflict with what Ali believes.

Citizenship

Citizenship is a statutory part of the curriculum at Key Stages 3 and 4 and a National Curriculum Foundation subject. It must therefore be taught. It has three strands: social and moral responsibility, community involvement and political literacy.

In Citizenship students learn about, discuss and reflect upon issues within the social, legal, political, economic, spiritual and cultural spheres. They learn about areas such as fairness, social justice and democracy. Over the key stages, students are expected to take more responsibility and have greater involvement within the school, neighbourhood and community. The pedagogic approaches which are effective in this area will be similar to those employed within PSHE. Many schools deliver Citizenship in similar ways to PSHE and indeed, may conflate the two. Some schools use dedicated, and trained, teachers of the subject and allocate specific timetabled lesson to citizenship.

Citizenship is teacher assessed at Key Stage 3 through attainment descriptors. At Key Stage 4 there are both GCSE short courses and full GCSE available. Attainment in Citizenship must be reported to parents at least once a year.

As with PSHE, the issues for you as a beginning teacher are centred on ensuring that you have the knowledge you will require and in adopting appropriate teaching strategies which will allow, encourage and support students in expressing their views and learning to listen to and accept the views of others. You need, too, to recognise the links to other parts of school life here. If there is a school council, how can you encourage and develop effective participation for your form group? What opportunities are there for community involvement, both in the immediate neighbourhood and nationally? What links are there with other subject areas?

PRACTICAL TASK PRACTICAL TASK PRACTICAL TASK PRACTICAL TASK PRACTICAL TASK

Moving on

Develop an assessment framework and method of recording students' achievements for the lessons you teach in both PSHE and citizenship.

Frequently asked questions

I am not religious and never have been, and my placement school is not a faith school. Surely I am not expected to teach pupils to be spiritual? I object to this on the grounds that I do not personally believe in religions.

You need to reassess what you understand by 'spiritual development'. Ofsted is quite clear that 'spiritual' and 'religious' are not synonymous. Opportunities for spiritual development arise in all areas of the curriculum, and it is your legal responsibility to support the spiritual development of the pupils in your care, as it is for their moral, social and cultural development. Talk to your mentors about how you can do this in ways that are compatible with your approaches to teaching; but remember that professionalism does not always support our personal beliefs and values. Your job is to uphold the values of the school where you are teaching; if this is so incompatible with your personal beliefs that you cannot do it, then teaching is not the profession for you.

> *My subject does not use pedagogic approaches which require discussion in small groups and debate. I have never used role play or drama. I do not feel able to use these approaches. Where can I find help?*

You need to discuss these issues with your mentor and then take action. You could try observing teachers in other subject areas who do use these approaches, looking very carefully at how they set up groups and facilitate and encourage discussion. You will find that many of the skills needed to facilitate discussion (questioning, for example) are ones you already hold. You could also try pairing with a fellow trainee or your form's usual tutor to plan and, if possible, team-teach a session or sessions early in your training in order to give you the confidence and experience you need. Follow this, later in your training, by joint planning with you delivering the lesson and then move towards independent planning and teaching. Finally, read about strategies you can use to develop drama in the classroom (ask a drama colleague for advice) and also about circle time techniques.

A SUMMARY OF **KEY POINTS**

> **Make sure you understand how SMSC, PSHE and Citizenship are delivered in your placement school.**

> **Ensure that you develop your subject knowledge for PSHE and Citizenship where necessary.**

> **Make sure you are familiar with the PSHE and Citizenship curricula.**

> **Plan opportunities for SMSC in your teaching.**

> **Consider the pedagogical approaches which are appropriate for delivering these subjects.**

REFERENCES REFERENCES **REFERENCES** REFERENCES REFERENCES REFERENCES

Ofsted: *Promoting and evaluating pupils' spiritual, moral, social and cultural development*. www.ofsted.gov.uk/assets/3598.pdf

QCA (2005) *PSHE Key Stage 1–4: Guidance on assessing, recording and reporting*. QCA/05/2183

FURTHER READING FURTHER READING **FURTHER READING** FURTHER READING

Advisory Group on Citizenship (1998) *Education for citizenship and the teaching of democracy: Final report of the advisory group on citizenship* (The Crick Report). London: QCA.

Qualifications and Curriculum Authority (QCA) and Department for Education and Employment (DfEE) (1999) *Citizenship.* London: QCA/DfEE.

Useful websites

Teachernet: www.teachernet.gov.uk/pshe/listSection.cfm?sectionId=79
   Provides training, development and professional support for teachers

BBC Schools Key Stage 3 Teachers PSHE page: index on online resources for teachers of KS3 www.bbc.co.uk/teachers/keystage_3/topics/pshe.shtml

PSHE Association: www.pshe-association.org.uk

   Provides advice and information to teachers of PSHE

www.teachernet.gov.uk/teachingandlearning/subjects/citizenship

www.qca.org.uk/citizenship

   Two sites to provide professional support to teachers

www.teachingcitizenship.org.uk

   A website by teachers of citizenship to support teaching

www.citizenshipfoundation.org.uk

   Funded by business and other partners and devoted to raising standards of teaching of citizenship

10
The broader curriculum

By the end of this chapter you should:

- have a clearer sense of how you and your department relate to the broader school curriculum;
- understand some of the key choices a school makes regarding the construction of timetables, curriculums and pupil organisation;
- understand how national and school-based cross-curricular themes are delivered and some alternative approaches;
- be familiar with a range of integrated curriculum models;
- recognise some of the ways school and community interact to the benefit of both;
- recognise how a school's systems, structures and ethos are established on a carefully evolved set of values.

This chapter addresses the following professional standards for QTS:

Q3a, Q6, Q8, Q15, Q17, Q18, Q19, Q32

Introduction

This chapter attempts to put your subject in the context of the curriculum and school as a whole, so that you develop more understanding of how various systems and structures give the school its sense of direction, its energy and its integrity.

There are many ways in which curriculums, timetables, subjects, teachers' roles and the relationship between the school and its community can be organised. One of the reasons why your training places you in more than one school is to introduce you to alternative approaches to school organisation.

Hidden curriculums

In Chapter 7 you were encouraged to think carefully about how your school manages behaviour, and how you would use this system with your own students.

CASE STUDY

Alternatives

In school A, Michael, a Year 9 student, has been caught with a small cube of marijuana in his pocket. He is summoned to the head teacher's office with his parents. Michael has never been in serious trouble during his secondary school career. His parents are active supporters of the school: they attend parents' evenings and make sure Michael does his homework and attends school regularly. After a brief statement from the head teacher, Michael is permanently excluded from the school. It is school policy that this

---

will be the punishment for any student in the school found in possession of any drug. A very similar situation occurs in school B. A well-behaved boy, James, also in Year 9, is found in possession of marijuana. His parents are called in for an interview with the head teacher. He is severely told off; his parents are left in no doubt as to how seriously the school takes the misdemeanour; James is told that, if he is caught committing the same offence again, he will suffer more serious punishment, but, since his behaviour has always been good previously and because he understands the gravity of his wrongdoing, on this occasion there will be no further action taken against him.

These examples illustrate very different disciplinary 'systems'.

- What are the principles on which they are based?
- What do they indicate to you about these two schools?
- Where do they stand regarding current educational policies and practice?
- What do they tell you about the values of your current school?

REFLECTIVE TASK

- How, within the school's behaviour management system, will you endeavour to exemplify fairness and consistency?
- How will you establish good relations with a student whose behaviour has been very bad?
- How will you establish warm and trusting relationships with your students while maintaining an appropriate 'distance'?
- How, in your classroom and around the school, will you try to add to students' 'cultural capital'?
- How much of 'yourself' will you share?

Your manner with your students, how you address them and what you choose to share with them, even how you dress, are important factors in their educational experience. In the school context, we are all a model of behaviour for them, an example that they might try to emulate.

Teacher involvement

Although you are at the start of your teaching career you will have a great deal to offer the whole school in terms of ideas concerning, particularly, learning and teaching, and you will have plenty of energy. You will need to consider the means by which you can make a positive contribution, even at this very early stage, to whole-school development.

PRACTICAL TASK PRACTICAL TASK PRACTICAL TASK PRACTICAL TASK PRACTICAL TASK

You will almost certainly feel more comfortable observing staff discussions than taking part in them. But you will find attending staff meetings informative and might like to join a working party if only to listen to debate about curriculum development. Find out (from your subject mentor) the following.

- What is the role of the staff meetings and morning briefings?
- Is the work room/marking room a 'silent' area used solely for the stated purpose?
- Who uses the staffroom (all teachers? The head teacher? Senior staff?)

- Is there a system of working parties, developing policy and practice in key areas of the curriculum?
- If so, what is the membership? Is access open? Is representation from across the school, irrespective of age and experience?

The opinions and priorities of more experienced colleagues will be based on lengthy periods of teaching, discourse and analysis. While this should be properly respected, you will develop your own sense of what is right and what works in an educational context from involvement in school discussion and subsequent reflection.

Structures and school priorities

Every aspect of a school's structure is the consequence of choice. The relative size of classes is an example.

- In which year in your present school are the classes smaller: Year 7 or Year 10?
- Why has the school made this choice?
- How large are the high- and low-attaining sets comparatively?
- Does the school have a number of classroom assistants?
- Are they all linked to specific statemented students?
- In which years are most classroom assistants based?
- What has the school based this decision on?
- If your school has large classes, is this because it is considered more effective for teachers to have more non-contact time (for preparation and marking) but slightly larger classes?

Departments and faculties

A secondary school will have many departments and these are often grouped into faculties. Important academic decisions might be made in heads of department meetings, or, if the school is structured in faculties, at heads of faculty meetings. If the latter is the case, your department may be represented at these meetings by a head of faculty.

In one school, for example, there might be five faculties:

- the arts and physical recreation;
- humanities (history, geography, citizenship, social sciences, religious education, personal, social and health education);
- English and modern foreign languages;
- science and design technology;
- maths and information technology.

REFLECTIVE TASK

In Key Stage 3, each of these five faculties might be allocated two half-day blocks of time into which heads of faculty organise their curricula and place their teachers. You will see immediately that whatever curriculum and timetable organisation a school adopts, a very explicit statement about priorities and values is being made.

- What are the advantages and disadvantages of a faculty system?
- What makes a five-faculty system particularly practical?

- Which subjects are difficult to place in a particular faculty? Why?
- Most schools have already adopted or are moving towards hour-long lessons, five in a day, 25 in a week. Why do you think this is?

Moving on
- Plan your own faculty system, using as many faculties as you think appropriate.
- Are you allocating time fairly?
- Where have you put RE? MfL?
- Have you separated the elements of PSHE?

Now, analyse what values are embodied in your model: are these the educational values on which you would wish your curriculum model to be based? If not, try again.

Student organisation

Schools group their students by one set of criteria or another.

Some use bands: students are placed in one of two or three permanent bands. All their learning occurs in this band but, within their band, they join classes of different levels of attainment for particular subjects.

Some use sets: in this system students are grouped for each individual subject dependent on their current attainment levels.

Some use mixed-ability groupings, organising classes so that students carefully selected from across the attainment range are taught together.

Schools also have a special needs department for those students in need of more specialist support for their learning. It is common policy for students with special needs to be integrated into main school in those subjects they can manage and when opportunities arise.

Among the variations to these models are: express streams, withdrawal groups, 'extra' curricula for the gifted and talented and the use of learning support assistants for students with particular statements.

Many schools use a mixture of systems; for example, using mixed-ability arrangements for part or all of Year 7 in some subjects.

PRACTICAL TASK PRACTICAL TASK PRACTICAL TASK PRACTICAL TASK PRACTICAL TASK

Talk to the member of staff who writes your school's timetable and identify what are its main structures and priorities.
- Does the school operate a faculty system?
- Do the large departments teach a whole-year group at one time or are they 'paired' with another department?
- Why does your school favour the 'whole-school' or 'paired' approach?
- Can a student be easily moved to a higher set if his or her attainment goes up or a lower set if it goes down?

- Does the school have a learning and teaching policy statement?
- How does the member of staff in charge of timetabling take into account the differing requirements of heads of department when writing this complex but definitive document?
- What are the gender and ethnic profiles of the high-attaining and low-attaining sets?

Moving on

As you get to know the school better, consider what the timetable and relative class sizes say about your school's principles and priorities.

The school library

The library is often called the Learning Resource Centre to emphasise its importance to pupils' education and the role it plays in the development of independent learning.

PRACTICAL TASK PRACTICAL TASK **PRACTICAL TASK** PRACTICAL TASK **PRACTICAL TASK**

Over a week in mid-term visit the library whenever you can and by observation and questioning (of the librarian, teachers and students) conduct a survey using the following questions.

- Where in the school is the library located?
- Is there a full-time (before and after school?) librarian?
- Are there lessons given in how to use a library?
- How many fiction books?
- Non-fiction books?
- Magazines and newspapers?
- Computers?
- Books for staff?
- How is it decided what stock to buy?
- What displays are there in the library?
- Who sets them up?
- Are lessons taught in the library?
- Is there a system by which individual students can use the library during lesson time?
- Is there a policy of silence?
- Near silence?
- Is it practised?
- Who uses the library
- During lunchtime?
- After school?
- What for?
- Is it used for meetings?

Moving on

How important a role in students' learning does the library play? What are its role and status in the school? What do you think should be the role of the school library in the twenty-first century? How can the library best be used to develop students' independent learning?

Cross curricular themes (national)

Literacy, numeracy, and ICT across the curriculum, PSHE and Citizenship (see Chapter 9) might be delivered in your school in discrete timetabled slots; or they might be taught within other subjects. In some schools, learning objectives from some of the above subjects are allocated to appropriate subjects and it becomes the responsibility of those subject teachers to meet those targets in their lessons. In some, the tutor plays an important role in the teaching of areas like PSHE.

CASE STUDY

Language across the curriculum

Sally is given a placement in a school with a very keen and hardworking literacy co-ordinator. The school regards this as a key post for the development of learning and teaching. The co-ordinator has developed a system whereby the teaching of language is seen as the responsibility of all teachers in the school: the English department's curriculum for the teaching of spelling, grammar and text types is public knowledge across the school and co-ordination of this curriculum across all subjects is now expected. Sally teaches science and is very happy to recognise her role in the building of her pupils' specialist vocabularies. She is fairly confident that she can help deliver the school's spelling policy. But non-fiction genres defeat her. She is expected to reinforce what the English department has already done on Writing a Recount text and she doesn't know where to begin.

Sally discusses her concerns first with her subject mentor and then, at his suggestion, with the professional mentor. Her subject mentor is able to help her consider the main text types used in the teaching of science. The professional mentor, realising this is an issue facing many non-English teacher trainees, arranges for the literacy co-ordinator to run some twilight sessions for all the trainees placed in the school. The co-ordinator also recommends some reading and self-study books. Sally makes sure that she makes literacy a focus in her lesson planning so that her confidence is slowly built.

PRACTICAL TASK PRACTICAL TASK PRACTICAL TASK PRACTICAL TASK PRACTICAL TASK

Talk first to your subject mentor and your professional mentor about the school's policy and practice regarding language across the curriculum (LAC). Does a member of staff have specific responsibility for the development of LAC? Does your department have responsibility for the teaching or reinforcement of any areas of LAC? Is there a written policy? Is there any continuous professional development?

Make notes on the responses to these questions, and follow them up in the appropriate way. If appropriate, talk to the LAC co-ordinator. Plan to observe lessons in which LAC practice is good.

Curriculum integration

As with so many decisions that have to be made in a school regarding the curriculum and its delivery, there are advantages and disadvantages to integration. If citizenship is integrated, for example, it will be more difficult to arrange school visits and trips into the neighbouring community, or for local 'experts' to give talks in school. On the other hand, the more integration that takes place, the more the school is able to offer its students a coherent, interdependent learning experience. ICT and language are so integral to students' learning that it is vital that the development of these areas becomes the responsibility of all teachers.

Cross curricular themes (school-based)

In many schools there are examples of subjects working together, sometimes as a short, informal arrangement, sometimes as a semi-permanent feature of the curriculum. Two teachers might decide, as a consequence of a friendly discussion, that they will work together on a medium-term project. Perhaps an English and an art teacher will decide that their classes will produce an anthology of poems written in English and illustrations painted in art. A history teacher might join these two teachers and cover the historical background in her subject time. Such an arrangement, of course, is dependent on the same students being in the same class for the subjects concerned, and this is not a common scenario.

Displays, in the school foyer or library or in the assembly hall, of students' cross-curricular or single-subject based work are a useful means of sharing and stimulating learning, particularly if they are attractively presented and interactive.

A straightforward but effective arrangement is for the whole-school curriculum, at a certain point in the year, to be based on a particular, agreed theme, perhaps a theme like 'rebirth' or 'revolution', a theme that can have relevance and application in all or most subjects on the school curriculum. As the theme is examined and investigated across the school curriculum, the students' understanding can be deepened and given more substance. It might not be difficult to devise a whole-school curriculum based on a series of carefully ordered themes, as is the curriculum in Steiner schools.

Development of learning and teaching practice is often encouraged in a school through the concentration, across the whole school, on one or two agreed initiatives. The agreed focus might be 'purposeful small group work' or 'problem-solving', for example. The more democratically these 'learning themes' have been arrived at, and the more determined is the staff to embrace and master these pedagogical techniques, the more successfully will the school move towards becoming a fully fledged 'learning culture'.

In some schools, the students work to a set of learning objectives that function across all subjects in Key Stage 3. These are generic, learning-based learning objectives, focusing the students' attention on aspects of learning like planning for learning, collaborative learning and literacy and communication. They form a backdrop to the subject's own specific learning objectives, though some schools integrate the two sets so that students are presented with composite learning objectives.

CASE STUDY
Integrated curriculums
School A
In this school the curriculum is collapsed for a full two days during the spring term for all of Year 8. The students assemble in the hall, are given an introductory talk about irrigation and a detailed map of a region in Africa. They are introduced to a collection of building resources and put into groups of ten. They are told that they have until the following afternoon to construct a device for raising water to irrigate the surrounding area, based on which they will make a presentation. The students are to work on their own throughout the two days without teacher intervention.

After the two days the presentations are duly made and judged by an expert. A prize is given for the most effective solution.

School B
Normal curriculum is suspended every Friday for all Year 7 students and work is based on theme-based modules. The year begins with 'an election'. This module involves the students getting to know the school thoroughly, understanding the role of Member of Parliament and concepts like 'teamness', making speeches, writing manifestoes, taking part in 'Question Time', and holding an actual election. The second half of term 1 involves the writing (in rhyming couplets), preparation and presentation of a mediaeval mystery play. The students make all the costumes, props and scenery. The year continues with further modules, on the environment and a charitable enterprise and they all function within tight deadlines and conclude with presentations to 'real' audiences.

Students, in groups, are strongly encouraged to work independently, even having to secure resources using their own initiative. Learning objectives are taken from RSA's Opening Minds (see Useful websites).

School C
In this school, Year 7 students follow a fully integrated curriculum based on the core subjects, English, maths and science. Pupils stay in the same classes (tutor groups) throughout the timetable. They meet far fewer teachers than in most secondary schools and spend most of their lessons in the same room, their tutor room. The Year 7 curriculum is co-ordinated by the head of cross-phase links whose responsibility it is to maintain very close curriculum (and pastoral) links with the school's partner primary schools, particularly the primary school with the highest value-added scores. She ensures that curriculum and learning and teaching are coherent across Key Stages 2 and 3.

REFLECTIVE TASK

Consider the relative merits of these three approaches to curriculum integration. You will find that all three provide stimulating learning environments for the students. Which of them do you find has most to offer young learners?

Ask your mentor what cross-curricular activities are run by your present school and, if you can, read the paperwork and arrange to observe the practice. Ask some of the pupils involved their opinions of the experience. Why do you think schools try to develop cross-curricular work of this sort?

Extra curriculum

Whether or not extracurricular activities take place at lunchtime in your school will partly depend on the structure of a school's timetable. Some schools, for example, have a sliding lunchtime (to save time and space) with half the school taking lunch while the rest continue lessons. And, if a school has a wide catchment area, even after-school activities might be significantly curtailed.

Through inquiry and investigation, research the school's extracurricular programme and compose a thorough picture of all the opportunities offered the school's students.

- List the lunchtime activities currently on offer, for whom they are intended (years) and by whom offered (subject teacher).
- List the after-school activities currently on offer, for whom they are intended (years) and by whom offered (subject teacher).
- Which of these activities are most popular? Why do you think this is?
- List the productions (dramatic, musical, arts based) that the school has presented over the last five years.
- Describe the nature of these productions.
- Have there been any one-off extracurricular events in the school over the last five years (science weeks? literary weeks? French weeks?)
- What trips has the school organised over the last five years, both day trips and more lengthy visits, of leisure and educational purpose.

REFLECTIVE TASK

What does this additional curriculum tell you about:
- the nature of teaching;
- students' interests;
- this school.

What extracurricular activities might you like to offer, as a qualified teacher?

Other extracurricular activities

Productions are an excellent means of opening the school to the community at large. So are open days, or evenings, occasions when each department shows what its students study and how they learn, with displays of their work and the equipment, resources and activities they use.

Many schools raise money for a favourite charity, and parents and the wider public will be asked to play their part. Charity work gives students the opportunity to learn about PSHE in practical ways.

A healthy school will have close and continuous links with its immediate community. Local 'experts', police, ambulance drivers, gardeners from the local parks department, the fishmonger, economists from the finance department, will be integrated into the curriculum.

Pupils will visit local facilities, learn how the social networks function and study phenomena exemplified in the region. The library, in some schools, is the branch library for the local community, so members of the public use this part of the school frequently.

As all secondary schools develop their 'extended school' identity, more local services will be delivered on the school site. Schools will become much more integrated into community life and students and parents will feel closer to their school than they ever have.

A SUMMARY OF **KEY POINTS**

> Continue to observe the way your school deals with issues to do with behaviour and discipline so that you form a clear sense of the connection between values and school ethos.

> Find out, initially through your subject mentor, what are the main meetings and working parties, which ones you should attend and in which ones you should merely listen and in which you might contribute.

> Explore, initially through your head of department, the context in which your department operates: is it within a faculty system; how are the students organised; how is class size determined?

> Through observations and survey, consider the contribution of the school library to students' learning in the school.

> Through school-based research, explore the concept of integrated curricula and begin to develop your opinion of effective practice.

> Find out all you can about the school's extracurricular activities and consider their value to students' broader education.

REFERENCES REFERENCES **REFERENCES** REFERENCES **REFERENCES** REFERENCES

CSCS: University of Leicester, Moulton College, Moulton, Northampton. NN3 7RR.

Core Curriculum for Primary, Secondary and Adult Education in Norway. Norway: The Royal Ministry of Education, Research and Church Affairs.

Every Child Matters: www.everychildmatters.gov.uk

Rattansi, A. and Reeder, D. (eds) (1992), *Rethinking radical education*. London: Lawrence and Wishart.

FURTHER READING FURTHER READING **FURTHER READING** FURTHER READING

Apple, M. (2004) *Ideology and curriculum*. London: Routledge.

Claxton, G. (2002) *Building learning power*. Bristol. TLO Ltd.

Gardner, H. (1991) *The unschooled mind: How children think and how schools should teach.* New York: Basic Books.

Goleman D. (1996) *Emotional intelligence: Why it can matter more than IQ.* London: Bloomsbury.

Lucas, B., Greany, T., Rodd, J. and Wicks, R. (2002) *Teaching pupils how to learn.* Stafford: Network Educational Press.

Vos, J. and Dryden, G. (2001) *The learning revolution.* Stafford: Network Educational Press.

Useful websites

QCA www.qca.org.uk

RSA Opening Minds curriculum www.thersa.org/projects/education/opening-minds

14–19 diplomas www.14-19reform.gov.uk

Rethinking Schools Online www.rethinkingschools.org/publication

National College for School Leadership www.ncsl.org.uk

11
Making progress: observation, target-setting, assessment

By the end of this chapter you should:

- understand the purposes and formats of observation;
- know what is involved in the assessment of your progress towards the QTS Standards;
- be able to make the most of feedback and constructive criticism to help you make progress;
- know how to evaluate your own progress by reflecting on a wide range of evidence.

This chapter addresses the following Professional Standards for QTS:

Q7(a,b), Q8, Q9, Q29, Q32, Q33

Introduction

The purpose of this chapter is to help you understand how your progress is assessed and how you can best contribute to that process. One fundamental principle of assessment is to know exactly what the assessment criteria are, so you can prepare yourself as well as possible. If you know what is being assessed and how, you are more likely to be able to develop the skills, knowledge and attributes in order to be successful. As is the case when you are assessing your learners, assessment and evaluations you receive should help you to know how to make further progress in your professional development. This will, of course, be of benefit to you and to your learners. As a trainee teacher, you will be assessed against the QTS Standards or similar professional standards which apply to your situation, and depending on your programme, may also have work assessed against Masters level criteria.

Purposes and forms of observation

Your professional progress will be observed for many reasons, including:

- to provide support and training for you;
- to track your progress towards the QTS Standards (or similar);
- to set you individual targets in relation to the standards;
- to monitor your targets;
- to assess your planning, documentation and record-keeping;
- to provide feedback to you on all aspects of professional performance;
- to work with you in a constructive, sensitive way, with the aim of developing your professional competence.

Your teaching will be observed during your placements in a variety of ways.

- Most ITTPs will expect a regular, minimum number of full lesson observations with written and verbal feedback. These may be conducted by your subject mentor, professional (whole-school) mentor or a class teacher.
- The subject teachers of the classes on your timetable will mostly observe very frequently in a less 'formal' manner: perhaps by observing parts of lessons, teaching alongside you, 'popping in' to lessons, etc.
- Other senior teachers in the school may come in to see you teaching without announcing this as a formal observation.
- Your tutors from your ITTP will observe, usually jointly with a school-based member of staff at a prearranged time.
- You will probably also benefit from peer observation (i.e. other trainee teachers) either formally as a 'pair' or less formally.
- An external examiner may observe your teaching, perhaps as part of a 'sample' for moderation purposes or perhaps because there are concerns about your progress.
- Of course, you may also be seen by an inspector from Ofsted, either when your school is being inspected or when your ITTP is.

However, it is not only your lessons that will be observed. A crucial measure of successful teaching is the learners' progress. This can be 'observed' not only in lessons, but also through outcomes, e.g. via exercise books, homework and tests. Your professionalism will also be 'observed' by a very wide range of people. How do you conduct yourself around the school? How do you work and collaborate with colleagues? How do you go about your planning and assessment? How do you cope when communicating with parents/carers? How do you work with, for example, learning assistants or SEN support staff?

During your placements, think carefully how you will spend time in school when you are not actually teaching. Consider the impression you give to others if you only ever chat, drink coffee, read your private email or even fall asleep. Use this time productively – beneficial both for your time management and your professional image. There are always plans or resources to be made, or some equipment or ICT software to be investigated. Marking and other assessment are a valuable way to spend this time and also have the added benefit of an opportunity to ask if you encounter any problems. Other possibilities include arranging continued observation of your own and other curriculum areas at whatever stage in the placement (for example, class management in a very different subject to your own), subject classes not otherwise experienced, or a parallel class to one you are working with. It might also be possible to become more involved with the running of the school, for example by attending meetings, shadowing your mentor during various duties. These will certainly all impress your 'assessors', but more importantly will provide you with a wider professional perspective.

All these 'observations', whatever their form, contribute towards the assessment of your progress towards the QTS Standards. They also inform references, professional conversations with your colleagues, etc.

Each trainee is different and brings her or his own needs and strengths. All will benefit from observers' perspectives on your classroom, your ideas and resources and you will be helped to evaluate your own progress via their comments and questions. They, in turn, will be delighted with the input you may make in their department; and effective mentors and observers will dedicate a great deal of caring, professional time to you if you find learning to teach difficult for a variety of reasons. The expertise your observers have gained in their teaching and make use of in their feedback is extremely valuable to you.

Preparing to be observed

Feedback you should expect: verbal and written (formal/less formal, school/ITTP).

Hopefully, whoever observes you should provide the following 'desirable' features to aid you in your professional development. Where this is not the case, you may have to take some action. Try to complete the column on the right as professionally as you can.

PRACTICAL TASK PRACTICAL TASK PRACTICAL TASK PRACTICAL TASK PRACTICAL TASK

Desirable features of feedback	How you might address this if it is not the case
Takes place as quickly as possible after the observation so that memories are fresh.	Check when you will be receiving feedback when you know you are going to be observed.
Takes place in a quiet, private, interruption-free environment.	
Is there a careful, sensitive balance between support and challenge?	
Encourages self-evaluation and reflection by the trainee teacher initially. Typical opening questions might be: • What did you think about the lesson? • What went well and why? • What might you have done better or differently next time? • How typical was this lesson with this particular class? • Were learning objectives met?	
Is honest and constructive.	
Is challenging but not threatening.	
Establishes a small number of clear, agreed targets for future development. These should be linked to the QTS standards if possible.	
Where a lesson has been unsatisfactory, results in professional, constructive dialogue, not personal criticism.	
Helps you to identify strategies for improvement and make practical suggestions.	
The observer and you as the trainee teacher each sign the lesson observation record (or similar).	

Using feedback productively

After an observation and after receiving the feedback, you then need to engage in a process of reflection in order to make improvements. It is very tempting to focus only on the positive comments on the lesson observed and to gloss over any criticism; it is probably more common to dwell on the criticism and not realise you are also making progress. Of course the ideal lies in a balance between the two: allow yourself to acknowledge what has gone well and what you have achieved, but at the same time focus on the reality as objectively as you can and see how you need to improve for next time. If you find yourself being too hard on yourself, make a conscious effort to look for positive comments. If you have received written feedback, use a highlighter pen to pick out the elements that went well. If you tend to 'pretend' there is 'no problem', try to answer some key questions which are almost impossible to answer 100 per cent positively.

- Did all learners make the most progress they could have done?
- Was I fully aware all the time of how learners were reacting and how engaged they were?
- Would all learners be able to answer confidently what they now need to do in order to make further progress?

Whilst most mentors and teacher observers are very supportive and constructive, there may be occasions when this is not the case. Even if your observer is excellent, when you receive feedback, you might find some of it quite difficult to accept. Some points you may tend to disagree with, for example: (a)*You ignored the boys during this lesson and focused entirely on the girls*; some points you may find upsetting, for example: (b) *I felt you had no presence in the classroom and the pupils were able to get away with doing almost nothing productive*; some you may not understand, for example: (c) *I found your plan and its execution did not cater for the diverse needs in the class*. It is when this happens that the relationship between you and the observer becomes very important (see Chapter 2). You need to respond to such potential points of conflict positively and professionally. It is not productive or beneficial to your development if you respond defensively without any reflection.

REFLECTIVE TASK

How do you envisage you might respond to feedback such as (a), (b) and (c) above?

Work out how you might respond in a constructive manner that enables you to make progress without creating problems with colleagues.

For example, some suggestions might be as follows.

(a) Ask for concrete examples of when and how you did this (e.g. was it in a specific activity? Was it because the girls were vying for your attention and you found this difficult to deal with?) Then you could suggest ways in which you might work on this next time and see what your mentor thinks.

(b) Try, although you may find this very difficult, not to take this personally! Ask for clarification of what the observer thinks the pupils did learn in the lesson and say how you assessed their progress. Find out if your observer could perhaps video you with this class so you can step back a little and observe yourself afterwards. What do you think of your voice, your body language, your (lack of) confidence? Could your observer suggest a teacher of the same class whom you might observe to see the differences? This is useful even if it is not in your subject area, and it could also be helpful to observe an Advanced Skills Teacher or Excellent Teacher.

(c) Explain to your observer what you think the diverse needs are in the class and ask whether he or she agrees with this, or if they could perhaps explain to you exactly what they mean by the diverse needs in this instance. Show them how you planned to differentiate in the lesson and how this may have not worked as intended in the lesson.

If there are a few areas of concern, perhaps ask your mentor to help you prioritise and focus on specific issues which should help you move forward (e.g. areas such as clarity of learning objectives, settling the class and the use of effective questioning).

In each case, try to gain something positive from all such situations: something to take away to help you plan for such occasions in the future.

Mostly, your observers will want to see how you listen to and act on advice, how you are able to evaluate your learners' progress and how you put advice into practice subsequently. There are countless strategies for dealing with situations which may arise in the classroom, whether to help all learners make progress with the content and skills, or whether to work towards a more positive atmosphere in the classroom, etc. You and your observers can work on strategies together: trying new ways out is what your observers want to see next time.

To this end, if you remain (or appear to remain) passive during feedback, your observers may be concerned that you are not taking any ideas or constructive criticism on board. You can alleviate this by asking questions, volunteering opinions on your own performance and that of the learners, making notes actively on what is discussed and suggested. A key action for you is to be proactive in seeking solutions to issues identified by your observers. For example, after an aspect of your professional development has been highlighted in a feedback session, you could:

- seek out any notes you already have on the relevant topic from ITTP sessions, school-based training, etc.;
- refer to any reading lists or recommended websites and see what suggestions you can find;
- discuss with other trainees or other colleagues what they have done in similar circumstances;
- ask if your mentor has any suggestions as to where or from whom you could seek advice on the issue;
- check back on any previous feedback you have had which may have contained relevant ideas;
- bring any ideas you collect by doing the above to your next meeting with your mentor to show how you have acted constructively;
- incorporate the most relevant ideas into your planning for next time and put it into practice during the lesson;
- if appropriate, 'signpost' these elements where necessary to your observer, so they are aware you have taken advice on board.

CASE STUDY

Richard was four weeks into his teaching placement. He felt that he was not making as much progress as he had hoped with a difficult Year 8 class and that his development was constrained by the presence of the usual class teacher. Richard felt that the teaching style he wanted to adopt was very different to that of the class teacher. The suggestions she made in feedback were based on her own style, philosophy and practice which Richard felt he did not share. However, he felt unable to develop his own teaching style because the usual class teacher was still in all his lessons. He found that the pupils still deferred to her and awaited her reaction to things.

Finally, Richard broached the issue of finding his own 'teaching persona' with his mentor. He was careful to remain professional and not criticise the class teacher but simply make the case that he would like the space to develop his own relationship with the class and discover his own teaching style. His mentor negotiated with the class teacher to leave Richard alone for the lessons the next week and for him to be formally observed teaching the class in the subsequent week. The mentor also helped Richard to reflect upon those elements of the class teacher's practice that produced effective learning and high standards of behaviour (see Chapters 4, 5 and 7) so that he understood that these things needed to be incorporated into his own lesson planning and delivery, albeit in a different style.

Being proactive

Continued, focused observation of others

You should see placements as an opportunity to develop as a professional and work towards achieving the QTS Standards. Learning to teach is not a linear route where you observe and then put what you have observed into practice. If you continue to observe in a focused way throughout your placements, it is likely to be very beneficial for your development. Once you have taught a class, for example, it is more useful to see them in a different subject, so you can identify any issues or strategies. Once you have seen that you have a particular problem, say in timing plenaries, it is likely that observing others more experienced at this would be of great help.

REFLECTIVE TASK

Think about how it might be useful for you to:

- observe good teachers;
- work with individual pupils and small groups of pupils;
- team-teach with an experienced teacher;
- team-teach where possible with a fellow trainee.

Recording your lessons on video

It is sometimes difficult to 'see' exactly what an observer means when you are receiving feedback. It's possible sometimes that you were so involved in the lesson that there were elements you did not pick up on or of which you were not aware. In these cases, it can be really helpful (if a little scary!) to have one or two lessons recorded on video. You can look at this later in private if you wish, or alongside your mentor. Once you go beyond the 'cosmetic' aspects (such as whether your hair was perfect), video recordings can be really useful for:

- recognising issues with your voice (tone, volume, etc.);

- identifying good or not so good use of body language;
- seeing which pupils were engaged, when and why;
- realising how long you actually spent on various elements of the lesson;
- other aspects of teaching and learning identified by your mentor.

Self-evaluation: focusing on the learners (becoming a grounded reflective practitioner)

Considering your strengths/areas for development

You will need throughout your placements to try to evaluate your own strengths and areas for development. Typical issues you will probably need to reflect on are:

- planning – how you can make it sufficiently challenging, supportive and engaging;
- what learning has actually gone on and who for;
- your own subject knowledge (e.g. content, confidence, making it accessible);
- how to deal with aspects of timing (e.g. pace, short/long lessons, late arrivals);
- behaviour management (e.g. finding a balance, being assertive, how to settle, how to get learners contributing, dealing with challenging behaviour/low-level disruption);
- motivation/engagement of learners;
- how you can help learners make progress and become more independent.

Setting your own (realistic and achievable) targets and monitoring your progress

When you are set targets by your mentor or other observers, it helps if you feel you understand the targets fully (what exactly is expected of you?) and even more so if you feel you have played an active part in the discussion leading up to the setting of targets.

To achieve this, when you meet to receive feedback try to ensure that you receive the following:

1. An agreed identification of your strengths.
2. Clear identification of your areas for development.
3. Opportunity to raise any concerns/queries.
4. Review of any previous targets.
5. Discussion of what is necessary for you to make progress.
6. Identification of new/revised targets.
7. Explicit illustration of any immediate specific targets.
8. Links to your progress towards the QTS Standards.

> ### REFLECTIVE TASK
>
> From the above list, items 1–8, reflect on your own ideal order for them to occur during feedback. It would be good to then share this list with your mentor or other observers.

Moving on

If you feel that the feedback and discussion are not helping you make sufficient progress, or if you feel that, in the later stages of training, your development has 'plateaued', you might wish to suggest topics for future meetings. This helps develop your own professionalism. Such topics might include:

- teaching approaches to particular topics;
- approaches to particular classes or individual pupils;
- assessment for learning;
- marking of pupils' work;
- statutory assessment and exam specifications;
- resources;
- lesson planning and forward planning;
- differentiation of work for pupils;
- questioning skills;
- creative approaches;
- improving pupil engagement;
- working with learning support assistants;
- subject knowledge development;
- improving your own lesson evaluations.

Tracking your progress towards the standards

You will of course be assessed by means of the QTS Standards or similar professional standards, and these should be used to track your progress. The guidance available helps pinpoint exactly what is required for improvement to take place. You will need to collate evidence of addressing the QTS Standards.

PRACTICAL TASK PRACTICAL TASK PRACTICAL TASK PRACTICAL TASK PRACTICAL TASK

Collating evidence and moving on

On occasion, and particularly as you move towards the middle and later stages of training, it would be useful to undertake a QTS 'stocktake'. Where are you at the moment in your progress towards their achievement? Most ITTPs will expect you to monitor your progress towards the Standards through reports, through electronic records, etc. but you can also be proactive in reviewing your progress during discussions with your mentors and through self-evaluation. It is worth your while spending some time at this stage reflecting on what you have achieved and what needs to be done from here. Some practical ideas and questions are given below.

- Review your teaching placement file. What evidence do you have of your ability to plan for effective learning?
- Are your lesson evaluations focused towards students' learning and setting targets for future planning, teaching and your own development?
- Relationships with pupils – how would you judge these? What could you do now to make things as positive as possible? What evidence is there of your being able to develop secure relationships with students?

- Your pupils' learning – how much progress are your pupils making? What could improve this (further)? What data and evidence do you have to support your judgement and how are you using baseline data to show progress and CVA? (See Chapters 3 and 6.)

- How could you gain and collate evidence from learners (oral and written) to support your own reflection?

- Assessment – how are you assessing pupils' learning? What feedback are you giving to them?

- Recording – what evidence do you have of pupils' progress and how systematic is it? What data are you collecting and with whom does it need to be shared?

- QTS skills tests (registration/completion).

- Subject knowledge. What do you need to work on? Have you made the improvements you wanted to?

- What areas of the QTS Standards do you still need to develop and acquire evidence for meeting?

- ICT – What could you plan now to help you achieve your targets?

- Jobs – if you haven't got one, what could you do now to help the process? Have a look at your CV and ask your mentor's advice too.

A SUMMARY OF **KEY POINTS**

> **Ensure that you understand the purposes and formats of observation.**

> **Consider what is involved in the assessment of your progress towards the QTS Standards and be proactive in tracking your progress.**

> **Make the most of feedback and constructive criticism in order to develop your teaching.**

> **Evaluate your own progress by reflecting on a wide range of evidence.**

FURTHER READING   FURTHER READING   **FURTHER READING**   FURTHER READING

Brooks, V., Abbott, I. and Bills, L. (eds) (2007) *Preparing to teach in secondary schools: A student teacher's guide to professional issues in secondary education* (2nd edition). Maidenhead: OUP.

Capel, S., Leask, M. and Turner, T. (2001) *Learning to teach in the secondary school: A companion to school experience*. London: Routledge Falmer.

Ellis, V. (ed.) (2007) *Learning and teaching in secondary schools* (3rd edition). Exeter: Learning Matters.

Petty, G. (2004) *Teaching today – A practical guide.* (3rd edition). Cheltenham: Nelson Thornes.

Useful websites

Teachers TV has several video excerpts which focus on NQTs reflecting upon their teaching www.teachers.tv/video/1517

Exemplification of the QTS Standards with guidance upon evidence for meeting the standards. Although aimed at ITTPs rather than trainees, this site may have some useful information for you in tracking your meeting of the standards. www.tda.gov.uk/patners/ittstandards.aspx

12
Your first post

By the end of this chapter you should:

- **know how to look for a job;**
- **understand the importance of choosing the right school;**
- **know what information you need to collect prior to applying for a job;**
- **know what makes a successful interview;**
- **understand the conventions in place when attending interview and applying for jobs.**

This chapter addresses the following Professional Standard for QTS:
Q7(b)

Introduction

The purpose of this chapter is to introduce you to, and give you an overall view of, some of the key issues that you will need to consider when you start applying for teaching posts.

Finding out about jobs and schools in the area in which you want to work

You will wish to start thinking about your first post well before you begin the application process. In a sense, the whole of this chapter is about 'moving on'.

Teaching posts are advertised in a number of different ways. Some of you may find yourselves being offered a job at your placement school. Others may hear of teaching post vacancies through word of mouth. However, the most common way in which teaching posts are advertised is through the *Times Educational Supplement* (TES). TES Jobs is a specific section of the TES which lists teaching posts both in the United Kingdom and abroad. Jobs appear online on a daily basis although the paper version of TES is published on a Friday. There are other websites which also advertise teaching posts.

When you read through TES Jobs or when you access their website, it is relatively obvious which jobs are suitable for newly qualified teachers (NQTs) and which are teaching posts for more experienced teachers. Most NQT vacancies will state clearly that the post is aimed at an NQT or will have 'MPS' (Main Pay Scale) next to it. In some cases, trainees may wish to apply for posts which carry an extra responsibility and a TLR (Teaching and Learning Responsibility) allowance but this is fairly unusual. If applying for a position in a state school, you should always check that a vacancy is paid on the MPS scale before you apply for a post.

PRACTICAL TASK PRACTICAL TASK **PRACTICAL TASK** PRACTICAL TASK **PRACTICAL TASK**

Find the details of teaching pay scales, by going online and checking with the teaching unions' websites. What can you expect to earn in your first teaching post?

Another way to find out about teaching vacancies is to register with teaching agencies who work directly with schools to help them fill teaching posts. You may want to do an internet search to find which agencies operate in your area.

Local authorities (LAs) also advertise teaching vacancies on their websites and organise teaching pools for which you can apply by filling in an application form. Some LAs organise recruitment fairs at the universities and you should attend these if you would like to find out more.

Teaching vacancies are also advertised by schools themselves via their websites.

PRACTICAL TASK PRACTICAL TASK **PRACTICAL TASK** PRACTICAL TASK **PRACTICAL TASK**

Go online and access TES Jobs. Do a search on secondary schools in your geographical area and in your subject specialism and see how many jobs come up. Read through the job description and person specification. How many of these jobs are aimed at NQTs? Save this search and sign up to email alerts which will inform you of new vacancies using the criteria you selected.

Choosing the right school

Before applying for a teaching post, the most important point to consider is what kind of school you want to work in. Indeed, the school you choose will make an enormous impact on the success of your NQT year and therefore your success in your future career. Do not underestimate the importance of choosing a school which shares your values and beliefs and a school whose ethos you can respect and help to mould (see Chapter 10). You should also consider a number of other important factors such as the level of support your school is able to offer and whether or not they organise a structured continuing professional development (CPD) programme aimed specifically at NQTs.

The bigger picture

There are many other areas to consider when choosing the kind of school you want to work in during your NQT year. One of the things you should do is find out as much information as possible about schools in your geographical area as you may find this restricts your choices. For example, you may live in an area where there are very few single-sex schools or you may live in an area which operates a system with middle schools (ages 9–13) and upper schools (ages 14–18).

You will also need to consider the type of school in which you would feel comfortable working. This reflection should be about your core educational values. What are your views on public schools? Would you consider working in an academically selective school? Would you like to work in an inner-city school? Are you especially keen to work in a school with a sixth form? Would you work in a single-sex school or a faith school? Would you work in a faith school if you were of a different faith from that of the school? Are you particularly interested in students with special educational needs? Would you like to work in a special school? What are your views on academies? Would you like to work for one?

Every school has its own challenges; there is no such thing as an 'easy' school to work in, especially for your NQT year. There are, however, a number of elements which you should consider before you make your choice. You should consider your strengths and areas for development first of all.

If you are considering a state school, is there a specialism you are particularly interested in? For example, if you are a drama specialist, you may want to join a school that has performing arts status as this will make it more likely that the school accords a special place to drama and that there are extra financial and curriculum resources aimed at raising the profile of drama and the performing arts.

You will need to develop your understanding of secondary schools and their differences if you are to make an informed choice.

PRACTICAL TASK PRACTICAL TASK PRACTICAL TASK PRACTICAL TASK PRACTICAL TASK

Do some research on academies. What are the advantages to a community of having an academy in its midst? What are the advantages to a school of becoming an academy? If you have the opportunity, visit an academy which has recently opened in your area. Contrast your research on academies with specialist colleges. You should also look at the contractual differences between LA contracts and academy contracts.

Other considerations

You should also address the issue of choosing the right school from a very practical stand-point. You may have childcare commitments which mean that commuting to another locality is simply not convenient. You should consider how far you are prepared to commute and look for jobs accordingly.

You should also consider the facilities you would expect from your first school and make sure you check they have those facilities, ideally prior to applying for the job or on the day of the interview. Examples of facilities you may wish to consider include:

- how the school day is organised;
- length of lessons;
- length of breaks and lunch;
- teaching in different classrooms;
- ICT facilities across the school;
- interactive whiteboards;
- textbooks in use in your department.

You should read the Ofsted reports of any school for which you are thinking of applying for a job, as this will help you tailor your application and find out more about the school itself.

Think about the schools you have visited and worked in so far. What aspects about these schools did you value and respect? What are the key characteristics of a school in which you would like to work? Complete Table 12.1 in as much detail as you can to clarify these thoughts and narrow the criteria and choices you will need to make when applying for jobs.

Table 12.1

Key characteristics	Characteristics which do not really matter to me
Example: I would not like to work in a faith school or a special school. I would prefer to work in a school which has a sixth form.	*I do not mind whether it is a single-sex or a mixed school.* *I will travel up to 20 miles to work in the right school.*

Applying for your first post

Once you have decided what type of school you want to work in, you should start looking for a vacancy. Before you apply for a post, it is ideal if you can arrange to visit the school and meet or talk to the head of department. However, be prepared when you phone up to arrange a visit to be told that the school/head of department is too busy to meet you as they have been flooded with interest in the vacant position.

The application form

Most secondary schools' application forms are very similar. They all include a section on personal details, education, current and previous employment, and references. You should always photocopy the application form when you receive it so that if you make a mistake, you have a spare copy to start again. Try to fill in the form as neatly as possible as schools, like any other employer, will expect you have taken care when completing the form. Some schools and LAs provide an electronic copy of the application form which will help you make sure you submit a clean and tidy application. Get a friend or a family member to proofread your application before you send it off.

The supporting statement or covering letter

The purpose of the covering letter is to sell yourself to the school. You should aim to describe not only your teaching experiences and teaching interests but also your personality. Schools are looking to employ a teacher who will form an integral part of the teaching staff; you will be a role model for young people and are expected to have excellent communication skills and interpersonal abilities. Schools will also look for examples of your commitment to your colleagues and students.

You should address the covering letter or statement to the head teacher and make sure you structure your letter in clear paragraphs. You should end your letter with a final statement such as 'I look forward to hearing from you soon and would be pleased to be invited to discuss these points further at interview.' You should also end your letter with the appropriate closing salutation.

A good covering letter will be no more than two pages long. It should be tailored to the post and seek to address the person specification. Broadly speaking, you should include the following key information.

- Why you want to work in this specific school.
- Your previous teaching experiences in terms of key stages and examination syllabi.
- What makes you an innovative and creative teacher.
- Your personal abilities in terms of organisation, communication, teamwork, innovation.
- Specific examples of your teaching principles and beliefs.
- Your interest in the personal, social and educational development of students.
- Your classroom ethos.
- Your extracurricular interests and participation in clubs at previous schools/your desire to run clubs in your first post.

PRACTICAL TASK PRACTICAL TASK PRACTICAL TASK PRACTICAL TASK PRACTICAL TASK

Draft your covering letter and ask a friend, family member or teaching colleague to read it through to check you have covered all of the points described above. Is there anything you have forgotten?

A successful interview

You can never be totally ready for an interview but there are many things you can do to prepare. The first thing to consider is the different formats of interviews for teaching posts.

Most teaching post interviews are half a day or a full day in duration. You will be expected to report to the school reception at around 8.30 am and you will leave at the end of the interview day having been told (generally) by the end of the day whether or not you have had a successful interview.

Most interview days will include the following phases.

- Introduction to the head teacher and other candidates; programme for the day is outlined.
- A tour of the school (accompanied by a member of staff or a student).
- An interview lasting between 30 and 60 minutes with a panel including the head teacher and another member of the leadership team and generally the head of department, and sometimes a governor.
- A lesson you will teach to a group of students.
- A considerable amount of time spent sitting in the staff common room while other interview candidates undertake the same process.
- Lunch with the other candidates or with staff in the school.
- Some schools may also ask a panel of students to interview you.

Obviously, interview day formats will vary from school to school. We have tried here to outline the most common formats. You should also remember that you are on interview the minute you step inside the school. You may be judged on how you address the receptionist, what you say to the person guiding you on the tour of the school, how you interact with other interviewees and with teaching staff in the staff common room. Remember to be polite and courteous to everyone as you want the school to see you at your best.

Planning a successful interview lesson

Most teaching interviews will include planning and delivering a lesson to a group of students. The time you are given to teach will depend on the school, with some schools asking you to prepare to teach a 15- or 20-minute lesson while others will expect you to prepare a 30- or 60-minute lesson.

Most schools will inform you of the topic and age group you are teaching in advance although it has also been known for schools on the day to give you 20 minutes to plan a lesson you will then deliver afterwards.

You will probably not be given any extensive information regarding ability or special educational needs of particular pupils. Remember, the school is looking to see you deliver an innovative and creative lesson which shows them your teaching talents. You should cover the usual points you would cover in any lesson including sharing appropriate learning objectives with students and showing the observer that your students have made progress during your lesson. No matter how short or long the lesson is, it is advisable to have a clear structure with at least the following three key parts.

1. Starter, preferably engaging all learners through the use of paired or group activity.
2. Main activity, in which you demonstrate/teach something measurable.
3. Plenary, in which students demonstrate they have progressed during your lesson.

This format remains true whether you are delivering a 15-minute lesson or a 60-minute lesson, so think carefully about what you can cover in a very short interview lesson.

You should also aim to create a lesson which is engaging and innovative. You may want to use technology to make your lesson more engaging but beware of creating extra stress and pressure for yourself if you are using technology in unfamiliar surroundings. Have a back-up plan ready in case the technology fails you (for example, the projector the school has organised for you does not work during your interview lesson).

Planning for the interview

There are many ways to prepare for an interview. The most effective ways are to consider how you would answer interview questions and to practise through a role play with a friend, colleague or family member to make sure that your answers make sense to whomever is listening to you.

Common interview questions
- Describe a situation where you dealt with a student's poor behaviour in your classroom.
- How would you deal with a student misbehaving in your lesson?
- What makes a good lesson?
- Describe a successful lesson you taught. What made it a success?
- Describe a lesson that did not go well. What did you learn from this experience?
- What are your strengths/weaknesses?
- Why do you want to work in this school?
- What can you bring this school?

- Why teaching?
- Where do you see yourself in two/five/ten years' time?
- What are your ambitions?

At the end of the interview, you may also be asked if you have any questions you would like to ask. This is a good time to ask any questions which have not been covered previously. You may want to ask the school what kind of induction programme they have in place for NQTs. You may ask whether you are likely to have a form group and what year it would be. It is a good idea to have a question ready to ask as it shows you are keen and interested in the school.

If you are offered the post, you will need to ask questions regarding pay if you are unclear about the salary. If you have previously worked in a related field, some schools and LAs will allow you to start on a higher point of the teaching pay scale but this is not automatically the case.

PRACTICAL TASK PRACTICAL TASK **PRACTICAL TASK** PRACTICAL TASK **PRACTICAL TASK**

Prepare your answers to the questions listed in this chapter. Get a friend or colleague to 'interview' you. Ask them to score you on your body language, your eye contact, whether your answers are convincing. Ask them to give you some advice on how to improve your interview technique. Remember: those who give the most confident interviews have practised beforehand.

Case Study

John has been applying for a few jobs during the second half of his training year. So far, he has been to two interviews but did not get past the lesson observation stage of the interview process. John is not sure what he has been doing wrong but has been discussing his interviews with his school mentor. It became clear that John was not showing himself in his best light when he presented himself for interview. John had been using materials from a well-known website for his lessons rather than developing his own resources. John's mentor felt that schools would want to see John planning his own resources and this was probably one of the key reasons he was not getting past the lesson observation phase of the interview. At his next interview, John prepared his own resources including two different worksheets for differentiation. The feedback he got from this lesson was very positive and he made it through to the interview stage of the application process.

Teaching post conventions

Teaching posts are a little different to vacancies in other sectors. It is very likely that the decision will be made on the day of the interview with regards to who will be offered the post. You will also be expected to decide as soon as you are offered the job whether or not you want to accept it. If you decide at any point during the day that you do not actually want to work in the school which is interviewing you, it is good form to withdraw immediately.

If you want to discuss the possibility of extra salary points due to your previous experience, it is good form to do so after you have been offered the post but before you have accepted it.

Frequently asked questions

Everyone around me has been applying for jobs and attending interviews but I have not even started thinking about it. Should I be worried?

Trainees often worry that there will be a job shortage if they do not apply for a teaching post early. This is a myth. Teaching vacancies appear any time from September to June but it is important to remember that the majority of jobs are advertised from February onwards. This is in part due to the fact that schools often make decisions regarding the curriculum and the timetable around this time of year and so new positions can be created at this time. You should start thinking about applying for a job any time from December onwards but do not worry if it is March and you have not started applying for a job yet. There is still plenty of time.

I have an interview on Monday for one school then another interview on Wednesday for the school I really want to work in. What should I do?

This is a very difficult situation to find yourself in as you will need to decide on Monday (if you are offered the post) whether to accept it. You cannot know whether you would be successful in the later interview. In some cases, schools have been known to let candidates wait until they have gone through the interview process at the second school before forma-lising their job offer but this is rare. You should consider carefully whether you would wish to work in the Monday school if you were unsuccessful in the Wednesday school. If the answer is 'yes', you may want to attend interview at the Monday school and see what happens. If you find you do not really want to work in the Monday school at all, it is good professional practice to withdraw.

I worked for a number of years in another job before deciding to be a teacher. Can I expect to start my career as an NQT on a higher salary?

Sometimes, you can be remunerated for your previous experience but do not expect to receive a higher salary automatically as LAs have very different procedures for regulating teaching salaries. It will depend on the school's own system as well as the LA's.

Will I be paid over the summer and/or will I receive some kind of recruitment and retention allowance for taking a job?

Some schools and LAs may offer to pay you over the summer or to include a recruitment and retention allowance as part of your salary, but be prepared that many schools do not follow this practice. Remember that depending on the type of school which you decide to join, your pay may not be protected by the Teachers' Main Pay Scale (for example, if you join an independent school or an academy).

I have an application form to complete but I am a little confused about who to put down as referees and whether or not to include my teaching placements in my previous employment record.

You should speak to your peers and your university tutor and subject mentor if you are unsure of how to complete the form. Most trainees provide a referee from your ITTP and a school referee, who would normally be your mentor. References are normally checked before interview and it is good practice to ask your referee before putting their names down on your application.

A SUMMARY OF **KEY POINTS**

> Before you apply for any job, you should think carefully about what kind of school you want to work in.

> Make sure you complete the application form thoroughly, neatly and professionally.

> When writing your covering letter, make sure you include not only your teaching interests and past experiences but also a section on your personal attributes.

> When preparing for interview, make sure you have rehearsed your possible answers and if possible, role play the situation.

> If you are asked to plan a lesson, make sure it covers at least three parts and that your students make progress.

FURTHER READING FURTHER READING **FURTHER READING** FURTHER READING

Hammond, Michael (2005) *Next steps in teaching: A guide to starting your career in the secondary school*. London: Routledge.

Useful websites

The most popular teaching jobs websites

    www.tesjobs.co.uk

    www.eteach.com

For information on pay and conditions in the teaching profession and lots of useful advice for NQTs use the teaching union websites listed below

    www.nut.org.uk

    www.naswut.org.uk

    www.atl.org.uk

All teachers seeking employment in England need to register with the general teaching council

    www.gtce.org.uk

For up-to-date government information regarding all UK schools and UK education policies

    www.dfes.gov.uk

For information on teachers' pensions

    www.teachersretirementagency.co.uk/

For information on types of school

    www.teachernet.gov.uk/educationoverview/uksystem/structure/schooltypes/

For information on academies

    www.standards.dfes.gov.uk/academies/what_are_academies/?version=1

The Specialist Schools and Academies Trust

    www.ssatrust.org.uk/

Appendix 1
Exemplar lesson plan pro forma

Previous targets set by mentors/tutors relevant to this lesson:

Class:	Date:	Time:	No. of pupils:	Level of ability:	No. with IEPs/ statements:	Support:

Context of this lesson (previous learning outcomes, group overview, place in SOW, aims of trainee re: own performance, and so on)

Learning objectives	National Curriculum references

Safety/Risk assessment

Assessment opportunities: strategies and criteria	Expected learning outcomes
During lesson	After lesson	

Differentiation strategies/Providing challenge

Balance of interaction:	Whole class	Pair work	Individual	Group
Learning styles:	Visual		Auditory	Kinaesthetic

Materials/Resources (in addition to 'classroom kit')	Homework Task: Assessment criteria; Due date:

ICT	Students:
Teacher:	

Cross curricular opportunities
Moral   Social   Cultural   Spiritual   Literacy   Numeracy   ICT

Planned flexibility

LESSON OUTLINE

Learning objectives		
Learning objectives to be shared with students	Expected learning outcomes	

NB: Number of activities is, of course, variable

TIME	ACTIVITY		Subject-specific language, key questions, key words
	Teacher (indicate key teaching points with **'TP'**)	**Pupils**	
	Objectives (indicate when these will be shared)		
	STARTER:		
	Homework setting		
	MAIN BODY OF LESSON		
	PLENARY		

Appendix 2
Exemplar medium-term planning sheet

Weekly/Medium Term Planning						
Class:		Unit/topic		Week beginning:		
Time available:		No. of lessons:		Teacher:		
Lesson/date	Material	Objectives		Possible activities	Assessment opportunities	Homework
Next week:						

Appendix 3
Lesson evaluation pro forma

Lesson evaluation

Ask yourself:	Yes	No	At times
Did the students meet the learning objectives?			■
If I were a lazy student in your class, could I have got away with doing very little?			
If I were a very able student in your class, would I have felt challenged?			
If I were a lower-ability student in your class, would I have felt lost or confused?			
If I were a shy student in your class, would I nevertheless have had chance to contribute orally in some way?			
If I were a hard-working student in your class, would I have felt praised and my achievement acknowledged?			
Would a student in your class be able to summarise what they had learnt during the lesson?			
Would a student in your class be able to describe how they could improve their learning?			■

Your comments on:	
Lesson start/STARTER	
Lesson end/PLENARY	
Instructions	
Transitions	
Activities	
Matching/differentiation	
Assessment – how?	
Involvement of all students?	
Timing	
Resources	
Your explanations of any questions/ misconceptions	
Pace	
Students' learning	
Students' behaviour	
Students' understanding of 'what they were supposed to do'	
Students' interest and involvement	
What subject difficulties do you think the students experienced?	

What was the best part of the lesson? Why?

Targets/action points for future lessons:
Teaching:
Learning:

Index